Welcome to the HealthyGirl community!

This accessible plant-based cookbook from the wildly popular vegan influencer Danielle Brown features life-changing recipes that will make you feel your best. These simple and approachable recipes will show you how to make nourishing meals that are free of animal products without making you feel like you're restricting yourself or missing out.

Transitioning to a plant-based lifestyle can seem intimidating, but when you're in the **HealthyGirl Kitchen**, plant-based eating doesn't have to be complicated. Danielle covers the entire food-prep spectrum, including breakfast, salads, soups, comfort food, dinners, desserts, and more!

The **HealthyGirl Kitchen** cookbook contains 100+ plant-based recipes that are free of refined sugar and flour, offer gluten-free options, and are ridiculously easy to prepare. Pretty soon you'll be savoring these fresh meals and telling your healthy besties all about it.

healthygirl

KITCHEN

Danielle Brown

healthygirl
KITCHEN

100+ Plant-Based Recipes to Live Your Healthiest Life

Publisher Mike Sanders
Senior Editor Alexander Rigby
Art Director William Thomas
Senior Designer Jessica Lee
Recipe Photographer Ari Brown
Lifestyle Photographer Amanda Julca
Recipe Tester Trish Sebben Malone
Proofreaders Lisa Himes, Lisa Starnes
Indexer Johnna VanHoose Dinse

First American Edition, 2023
Published in the United States by DK Publishing
6081 E. 82nd Street, Indianapolis, IN 46250

The authorized representative in the EEA is Dorling Kindersley
Verlag GmbH. Arnulfstr. 124, 80636 Munich, Germany

Published in the United States by Dorling Kindersley Limited

Library of Congress Catalog Number: 2022950173
ISBN 978-0-7440-7807-7

DK books are available at special discounts when purchased in bulk for sales promotions,
premiums, fund-raising, or educational use. For details, contact: SpecialSales@dk.com

Printed and bound in China

For the curious
www.dk.com

This book was made with Forest
Stewardship Council ™ certified
paper - one small step in DK's
commitment to a sustainable future.
For more information go to
www.dk.com/our-green-pledge

To my husband, Ari.

Thank you for encouraging
me to follow my dreams.

contents

breakfast

salads + bowls

comfort food

dinners

side dishes

hosting

desserts

my story

Every now and again you meet a lifelong vegan, but I am not one of them. I grew up eating meat, dairy, and eggs (a very typical American diet). I attended college at Michigan State University, a school that is well-known for its massive food court-like dining halls. As an unsupervised 18-year-old with unlimited dining hall access, I was like a dog without a leash. The MSU dining halls had an all-you-can-eat pasta bar, pizza, soft-serve machines, make-your-own omelet stations, ice cream cookie sandwiches, fresh baked goods, you name it. While this was fun for the first semester, I started to regularly feel sick after eating and the infamous freshman fifteen was creeping up on me. I knew I had to make a change. I wanted to "get healthy," but I didn't know exactly what that meant. Upon doing my own research, I stumbled across a plant-based diet.

When I first learned that a plant-based diet meant eating a vegan diet, this was unfamiliar and foreign to me. Didn't vegans smoke weed all day and eat tofu? I couldn't imagine meals without dairy—I was a cheese-a-holic. From feta cheese to soft-serve ice cream to cheesy pizza, I was scared to give up my favorite foods. In my college dorm room, I was forced to get creative. I started microwaving sweet potatoes, I made the salad bar my best friend, and I kept a huge bowl of fruit that didn't need to be refrigerated on my desk for easy snacking. Four months into plant-based eating, I lost weight, my skin became clearer, I had so much more energy, and my chronic heartburn disappeared. I realized that if I was able to learn how to eat a well-balanced plant-based diet in a dorm room, anyone could do it. I knew that I wanted to share my knowledge of plant-based eating with everyone who would listen. After graduation, I went to nutrition school and became certified as a holistic health coach.

Today, I share easy, nourishing, plant-based recipes with millions of people on social media. I share the tips and create the kind of recipes and meal ideas that I wish I had back when I first went vegan years ago. I am here to inspire you every day to fall in love with cooking (with plants as the star of your plate) and take care of yourself. It feels so good to eat foods that fuel you and nourish you.

how to use this book

I want you to view this book as your healthy (plant-based) eating bible. Whether you need easy dinners, ideas for what to make when you're hosting guests, breakfasts that fit into your busy schedule, or desserts that literally anyone could make, this book has it all.

Organize Your Kitchen

Cooking is much easier and more enjoyable when your space is organized properly. Keep your spices in jars with easy-to-read labels, have designated bins in your pantry for your most-used items, use mason jars or containers with labels to keep bulk items like rice and pasta, and get any clutter that doesn't belong in your kitchen, out. This is a game changer.

Prepare for the Week

Pick one day of the week that best fits your schedule to go grocery shopping. Sunday is typically the best day as most people head back to work on Monday. Choose the HealthyGirl breakfasts, lunches, and dinners you want to make for the week, and make a grocery list for the store.

Meal Preparation

If you have a busy schedule and prefer not to cook for every meal, when you're done grocery shopping, set aside a few hours to prep some meals in advance for the week. Some examples are keeping AB+J Overnight Oats and Mango-Mama Chia Pudding in the fridge for ready-made breakfasts, large batches of salads, No-Fish Tuna or Eggless Egg Salad for quick sandwiches, and recipes like the Meal Prep Fajita Bowls and a big pan of the Cheesy Girl Lasagna for dinners.

Equipment You'll Need

I encourage simplicity in the kitchen. You only really need a few staple cookware pieces, appliances, and utensils.

High-Speed Blender: A strong, powerful blender is a must-have in the kitchen for making great smoothies, smooth sauces, dressings, soups, and more. I bought my Vitamix in college, and we use it upwards of five times a day. A reliable, high-speed blender is the best investment.

Food Processor: You will notice that a lot of the recipes in this cookbook use a food processor. It serves a different use than a blender because often, a blender needs liquid to blend properly while a food processor doesn't. There are many affordable food processor options. I encourage you to get one.

Nonstick Pots and Pans: To keep cleanup time after cooking to a minimum, use nonstick pots and pans to prevent your food from sticking, making your life a whole lot easier. Nonstick pans also create less food waste. If your food is constantly sticking to your pan, you're going to be losing half of what you're making. However, make sure to get PTFE-free, nontoxic, nonstick pans.

A Solid Knife Set: I can't stress enough how important it is to have a sharp knife set. Chopping with dull, low-quality knives is not only frustrating but also dangerous. If the knife slips because it's dull, you can badly cut yourself. Do you already have knives, but they're dull? Simply order a knife sharpener.

Cooking Utensils: Keep a utensil jar on your counter or a utensil organizer in your drawer, and fill it with the essentials: a ladle, slotted spoon, whisk, rubber and wooden or metal spatula, and spaghetti spoon or pasta fork, as well as kitchen shears, wooden spoons, and tongs, just to name a few.

Kitchen Gadgets and Extras: a lemon juicer, peeler, grater, zester, set of mixing bowls, strainer, casserole dish, brownie pan, muffin tin, and set of cutting boards, as well as baking sheets.

Recipe Labels

Hey you! Refer to these shortcut labels that you'll find at the top of each recipe page. This cookbook is designed to be simple and user-friendly so you can navigate healthy recipe making with ease. Take a quick glance at the labels to see if the recipe is gluten-free, no-bake, soy-free, leftover friendly, nut-free, or if the meal can be made in 20 minutes or less.

gf	gluten-free	nf	nut-free
nb	no-bake	lf	leftover friendly
sf	soy-free	20	20 minutes or less

Please note that the gluten-free label refers to whether the recipe is inherently gluten-free; however, don't worry if you follow a gluten-free diet or have celiac disease, all the recipes are gluten-free optional. For example, when a recipe calls for a tortilla, pasta, or bread, you can always substitute a gluten-free version of that ingredient. A no-bake recipe will be a dessert or snack that doesn't require any oven or cooking time. A soy-free recipe does not contain soy. A lot of the recipes that contain soy can be changed to accommodate a soy-free diet. For example, if a recipe calls for soy sauce, simply use tamari or coconut aminos; both are amazing soy sauce alternatives.

I'm all about recipes that can be stored as leftovers and taste just as yummy reheated or eaten within a few days after making the recipe. You'll find the "leftover friendly" or "LF" label on the meals that can be enjoyed later as leftovers.

For anyone with a nut sensitivity or allergy, you will see a "nut-free" label on recipes that do not include nuts. Do you still want to make the healthygirl recipes that include nuts? Seeds are often a great substitute. For example, you can use sunflower butter instead of peanut butter, or hemp seeds as a cashew substitute when making a blended creamy sauce.

We all love a quick meal that can easily fit into our busy schedules. While the majority of the healthygirl recipes do not have you slaving away in the kitchen all day, the 20 minutes or less label is for those super-quick-and-easy recipes for when you don't have a ton of time to spend cooking.

why plant-based?

Eating a plant-based diet, which is closely related to the Mediterranean diet, is one of the healthiest, most nutrient-dense diets one can follow. A plant-based diet that focuses on whole foods, minimizing highly processed, packaged foods is optimal. There are vegans that still eat Oreos and frozen vegan pizza. While of course it's okay to treat yourself, the recipes in this book are based off a whole food, plant-based diet.

A plant-based diet has a *foundation* of fruits, veggies, nuts, seeds, legumes, beans, whole grains, and tubers (like potatoes and squash). A fully plant-based diet is free of meat, dairy, eggs, and fish. There is a common myth that it's not possible to receive adequate protein on a vegetarian or vegan diet; however, a plant-based diet offers all the necessary protein, carbohydrates, fats, vitamins, and minerals you need. Although there are fortified plant-based foods with B12, to be safe, taking a B12 supplement is encouraged.

Benefits of a plant-based diet:

- Prevents heart disease
- Lowers cholesterol
- Improves gut health
- Prevents constipation
- Helps maintain healthy BMI
- Lowers overall disease risk
- Helps maintain healthy hormone balance
- Reduces cancer risk
- Increases energy

Sources:

https://www.health.harvard.edu/blog/what-is-a-plant-based-diet-and-why-should-you-try-it-2018092614760

https://www.ncbi.nlm.nih.gov/pmc/articles/PMC3662288/

https://www.amdietetics.com/articles/how-can-diet-help-manage-pcos

https://www.hsph.harvard.edu/nutritionsource/soy/

https://www.healthline.com/nutrition/phytoestrogens-and-men

While eliminating all animal products may seem intimidating, this cookbook will show you how abundant, satisfying, and incredible your meals can be with plants as the focus. Whether you adopt a meatless Monday, start having plant-forward breakfasts, or commit to eating fully plant-based, the *HealthyGirl Kitchen* cookbook is here to be the go-to guide for your journey.

let's talk about soy

There is a common misconception that soy should be avoided and is not a health food. Soy contains isoflavones, which contains a type of estrogen called phytoestrogen (plant estrogen). Phytoestrogens are found in most plant-foods. There is little to no evidence that suggests phytoestrogens have harmful effects in humans.

Research has shown that women with breast cancer who consume soy products and food containing soy on a regular or daily basis had a 32 percent lower risk of their breast cancer recurring. This particular study, in the *Journal of the American Medical Association,* also reported that the women who consumed soy regularly had a 29 percent decreased risk of death from their breast cancer diagnosis, compared to women whose diet did not contain soy. Soy has also been shown across many studies to reduce prostate cancer risk by 26 percent.

Soy products such as tempeh, tofu, edamame, and soy milk are encouraged over highly processed soy products like soy-based meat substitutes. Soy-based meat substitutes are high in isolated soy proteins and may contain other ingredients that are not as healthy, and therefore could be harmful to one's health.

Including organic, non-GMO, minimally processed soy products in your diet, like tofu or edamame, are perfectly safe and healthy. Soy is extremely nutrient dense and is a great source of plant-based protein; it is a complete protein, meaning it contains all the essential amino acids. It's also an amazing source of potassium, fiber, magnesium, and B vitamins.

Be sure to consult with your doctor before making dietary changes.

go-to ingredients

Stock your fridge and pantry with these plant-based essentials. Buy ingredients like rice, quinoa, frozen fruit, pastas, etc. in bulk so you don't need to purchase them every time you go to the store. Items like olive oil and vinegars are staples that you probably already have in your pantry. This list will help you navigate the store with a plant-forward mindset.

Fruit:

Apples

Bananas

Blueberries

Butternut squash

Dried fruit: dates, figs, apricots, goji berries

Grapes

Kalamata olives

Kiwi

Lemons

Limes

Mangoes

Oranges

Peaches

Pineapple

Raspberries

Strawberries

Spaghetti squash

Tomatoes

Veggies:

Avocados

Baby spinach

Bell peppers

Broccoli

Cauliflower

Corn

Cucumbers

Kale

Mushrooms

Purple cabbage

Romaine

Root Veggies:

Beets

Carrots

Fingerling potatoes

Garlic

Onions

Russet potatoes

Sweet potatoes

Protein:

Black beans

Chickpeas

Lentils (green, red, brown)

Northern white beans

Protein powder

Tempeh

Tofu

Freezer:

Frozen fruit

Frozen peas

Frozen shelled edamame

Frozen veggies

Grains + Flours:

All-purpose gluten-free flour

Basmati rice

Brown rice

Chickpea flour

Gluten-free pasta

Jasmine rice

Quinoa

Rolled oats

Short-grain rice

Sourdough bread

Sprouted whole-grain bread

Whole-grain pasta

Whole-grain tortillas

Whole wheat flour

Condiments + Sauces:

Balsamic vinegar

BBQ sauce

Full-fat coconut milk

Coconut aminos

Hot sauce

Ketchup

Mustard (yellow + Dijon)

Nutritional yeast

Olive oil

Red wine vinegar

Soy sauce

Tahini

Veggie broth

Nuts + Seeds

Almond butter

Almonds

Chia seeds

Flaxseed

Hempseed

Peanut butter

Pecans

Pumpkin seeds

Sesame seeds

Sunflower seeds

Walnuts

Fresh Herbs:

Basil

Chives

Dill

Parsley

Rosemary

Sage

Thyme

Dried Herbs + Spices:

Chili powder

Cinnamon

Coriander

Cumin

Dried basil

Dried oregano

Dried rosemary

Dried thyme

Garlic powder

Ginger

Nutmeg

Onion powder

Paprika

Pepper

Red pepper flakes

Sea salt

Turmeric

Natural Sweeteners:

Coconut sugar

Maple syrup

Pure stevia extract (no additives)

who is a healthygirl?

Anyone can be a **healthygirl**, whether you're vegan or not, everyone is welcome in this community.

A **healthygirl** is the girl who wants to try having meatless Mondays, or who wants to start cooking healthier dinners for herself.

A **healthygirl** is the girl-on-the-go who needs quick lunch ideas that not only are good for you but also taste good too.

A **healthygirl** is the busy mama who wants to learn how to make healthier, plant-forward meals for her family.

A **healthygirl** is the girl who has no clue how to eat healthy (or how to cook in general), but wants to learn.

A **healthygirl** is the girl who wants to cook healthy meals with her partner. (Trust me, they're going to be obsessed with HGK recipes.)

A **healthygirl** doesn't restrict or deprive herself of food; she loves nourishing her beautiful body.

A **healthygirl** is the girl who wants to get out of a slump and start taking control of her health and happiness.

A **healthygirl** is the girl who wants to fall in love with cooking for herself, and this book will teach her how.

Sample HealthyGirl Meal Plan 1:

Breakfast: Clean Green Smoothie (page 28)

Lunch: Taco Salad (page 58)

Snack: Hot Girl Hummus (page 131)

Dinner: Easy Chickpea Coconut Curry (page 167)

Sample HealthyGirl Meal Plan 2:

Breakfast: Girl-on-the-Go Breakfast Burrito (page 47)

Lunch: Green Goddess Bowl (page 69)

Snack: Yogurt Parfait To-Go (page 136)

Dinner: Peanut Veggie Stir-Fry (page 163)

Sample HealthyGirl Meal Plan 3:

Breakfast: AB+J Overnight Oats (page 35)

Lunch: Fall Harvest Salad (page 57)

Snack: DIY Trail Mix (page 124)

Dinner: Kale Caesar Salad (page 50) and Life-Changing Baked Mac + Cheese (page 153)

Sample HealthyGirl Meal Plan 4:

Breakfast: Mango-Mama Chia Pudding (page 32)

Lunch: Greek Pasta Salad (page 65)

Dinner: Anti-Inflammatory Lentil Soup (page 84)

Dessert: Famous Chickpea Brownies (page 246)

about the author

While most kids watched Cartoon Network, I was glued to the TV watching Food Network. I idolized Rachael Ray. I used to pretend to be her, and I'd perform cooking shows for my family. I'd make random concoctions, often wasting my mom's spices, but she let me explore my curiosity for cooking ever since I was about eight years old. I've always been a foodie. (I never understood kids who were picky eaters.) The home videos of me shoving chocolate cake in my mouth from my first birthday can confirm this.

When visiting my friends' houses, it confused me when their parents would bribe them to finish the food on their plates. I was proudly a consistent, full-time member of the clean plate club. I never dreamed of being a chef, nor do I consider myself one today. I am just a girl who loves cooking and being in the kitchen. I don't measure anything when I cook; I'll add a little bit of this, a little bit of that. Let's just say I measure with my heart—especially garlic, you can never have too much garlic.

I live in sunny, gorgeous Boca Raton, Florida, with my handsome, supportive, vegan husband, Ari. I love long walks, candles, the ocean, cooking while listening to bossa nova jazz, dancing, any meal that involves pasta, chocolate, stuffing popcorn in my mouth, and snuggling under the covers with a cup of tea while watching movies.

My goal is that this cookbook will have a permanent place on your kitchen counter—use it in good health.

xo,
Danielle

healthygirl breakfast

start your day off right, bestie

superfood smoothie bowl

SERVES 1

One of my favorite activities is getting a smoothie bowl from a local juice bar. The only problem is that they're always super expensive. I learned how to make my own, and they taste even better than ordering a smoothie bowl out. It's yummier, so much more fun, and more cost effective to make your own smoothie bowls, besties.

prep time:
10 minutes

½ banana

1½ cups frozen mixed berries

¾ cup frozen pineapple

½ cup almond milk

Toppings:

½ banana, sliced

Berries

Shredded coconut

Granola

Hempseed

Peanut butter

1. In a food processor or blender, combine banana, frozen mixed berries, frozen pineapple, and almond milk. Blend until smooth. Only add more milk if needed—you want it to be as thick as possible.

2. Pour into a bowl and add on the toppings!

gf · sf · nf · 20

clean green smoothie

SERVES 1

Why do I feel like green smoothies have a bad reputation? My version of a green smoothie tastes like a tropical drink you'd order at the beach on vacation. If you need a boost of energy in the morning and want to feel super hydrated, this refreshing clean green smoothie will make you feel amazing. The secret weapon hidden inside is fresh ginger. Ginger aids in digestion, calms nausea, eases period pain, and boosts immunity.

prep time:
5 minutes

1 cup frozen pineapple

1 cup frozen mango

1 cup fresh spinach, lightly packed

1-inch piece fresh ginger, peeled and roughly chopped

Juice of 1 lime

2 tbsp hempseed, plus more for garnish

1 cup coconut milk

1. To a blender, add all the ingredients and blend until smooth, adding a few tablespoons of water if necessary.

2. Pour into your favorite glass and garnish with a sprinkle of hempseed.

gf   sf   20

peanut butter cup smoothie

SERVES 1

This smoothie tastes like an actual peanut butter cup. It's thick, creamy, cold, naturally sweetened with dates, and takes five minutes to whip up. Once your bananas are ripe, peel them, then add them to a bag or container in the freezer. This way, you always have a frozen banana ready for smoothie making. Frozen bananas are the key to a thick smoothie that has the consistency of a milkshake.

prep time:
5 minutes

1 frozen banana

1 scoop vegan chocolate protein powder

1 tbsp unsweetened peanut butter

1 Medjool date, pitted

½ cup nut milk

1 handful ice

Toppings:

Cacao nibs or mini dark chocolate chips

Oats

Peanut butter drizzle

1. To a blender, add all the ingredients and blend until smooth.

2. Pour into your favorite cup and drink up, healthy bestie.

mango-mama chia pudding

SERVES 1

Mornings are busy and hectic, sometimes too busy to make breakfast for yourself. This is a breakfast you prepare the night before so it's ready to go when you wake up. You should eat more chia pudding if you want to prevent constipation and increase energy. If you are one of those people who doesn't like to eat a ton in the morning but still needs something nourishing, this is the perfect light breakfast.

prep time:
10 minutes

refrigerate:
overnight

1 cup sliced mango (fresh or thawed from frozen)

3 tbsp chia seeds

¾ cup unsweetened nondairy milk

1 tbsp maple syrup

1 tsp pure vanilla extract

Toppings:

Shredded coconut

Hempseed

Fresh mango

1. In a food processor or blender, blend the mango until it forms a smooth purée.

2. In a jar or container, combine the chia seeds, nondairy milk, maple syrup, and vanilla.

3. Pour the mango pureé in the chia mixture and stir.

4. Top with shredded coconut, hempseed, and fresh mango.

5. Store in the fridge overnight, and enjoy in the morning.

ab+j overnight oats

SERVES 1

It's safe to say I like overnight oats *way* more than hot oatmeal. It literally tastes like dessert. The best part about overnight oats is that there's zero cooking involved. I suggest prepping three jars at a time for the easiest breakfasts. The complex carbohydrates in the oatmeal will help keep you full for hours, and the almond butter on top is filled with healthy fats, which support healthy hormones, hair, skin, and nails.

prep time:
10 minutes

refrigerate:
overnight

½ cup rolled oats

½ cup nut milk

2 tsp chia seeds

¼ cup dairy-free yogurt

1 tbsp maple syrup

1 tbsp jam

1 tbsp almond butter

Toppings:

Sliced banana

Hempseed

1. In a jar, combine the oats, nut milk, chia seeds, yogurt, and maple syrup.

2. Top with a layer of jam and a layer of almond butter.

3. Refrigerate overnight.

4. In the morning, add optional toppings (if using) and enjoy!

apple cinnamon baked oatmeal

SERVES 4–6

Regular oatmeal is good, but baked oatmeal is next level. If you haven't tried baking your oatmeal yet, you're missing out. This tastes like apple pie mixed with a cinnamon roll (um, yes please!) Bake a pan for the week, cut into squares, and reheat in the morning. This is also perfect for hosting a brunch. Eat it warm out of the oven—you will thank me later!

prep time:
10 minutes

cook time:
40 minutes

1½ cups nondairy milk

½ cup maple syrup

⅓ cup almond butter, plus more for topping

1 apple, peeled and diced

2 tsp pure vanilla extract

2 cups rolled oats

1 tbsp ground flaxseed

1 tsp baking powder

2 tsp ground cinnamon

½ tsp sea salt

1. Preheat the oven to 350°F (175°C). Grease a 9 x 9-inch baking dish or line with parchment paper.

2. In a large bowl, mix the milk, maple syrup, almond butter, apple, and vanilla. Add the oats, flaxseed, baking powder, cinnamon, and sea salt. Stir until well combined.

3. Pour the mixture into the prepared pan, and spread it out so it's even. Bake for 40 minutes. It should be firm on top when done and not wet.

4. Drizzle almond butter on top if you're feeling extra fancy.

5. Let cool for 5 minutes before cutting into squares for serving. It is best served warm. Cover and refrigerate for up to 4 days.

sf   nf   20

elevated avocado toast

SERVES 1

Avocado toast is a classic—am I right? There are some tricks to make the absolute best avocado toast. One of them is using high-quality bread like a seedy multigrain. Adding greens or sprouts on top adds nutrients and flavor. The creaminess of the avocado, sweetness from the balsamic glaze, crunch of the toasted bread, and spicy heat from the red pepper flakes make the perfect avocado toast.

prep time:
5 minutes

cook time:
2 minutes

1 ripe avocado

2 slices multigrain bread

Microgreens or sprouts

Balsamic glaze

Red pepper flakes

Sea salt

1. Scoop the avocado flesh into a bowl. Using a fork, mash until the avocado is mostly smooth with a few chunks remaining.

2. Pop the bread in the toaster, and toast to your liking. (I prefer medium-toasted bread.)

3. Spread the mashed avocado evenly on each piece of toast. Top with microgreens, and drizzle with balsamic glaze. Sprinkle on the red pepper flakes and sea salt. Enjoy immediately.

hummus toast

SERVES 1

Two of my favorite foods on Earth are hummus and bread. So why not combine the two to make the perfect combination? The Jewish girl in me screams when I make this because the flavors remind me of being in Israel. In addition to this brekkie only taking five minutes to make, it tastes like heaven.

prep time:
5 minutes

cook time:
2 minutes

2 slices bread

1 tbsp olive oil

1 tsp za'atar

¼ cup **Hot Girl Hummus** (page 131)

1 medium tomato, sliced

1 small cucumber, sliced

Salt and pepper, to taste

1. Toast two slices of your favorite bread. I like sourdough!

2. In a small bowl, mix the olive oil and za'atar.

3. Spread Hot Girl Hummus on each slice of toast.

4. Top with tomato and cucumber slices.

5. Drizzle with the za'atar mixture, and season to taste with salt and pepper.

morning goodness muffins

SERVES 12

What could be better than a fluffy, moist, perfectly sweet muffin that's 100 percent gluten-free and vegan? This healthy muffin is sweetened with coconut sugar and maple syrup, which have a lower glycemic index than white table sugar. It's almost impossible to find a light gluten-free muffin that isn't dense, so I tried my best to create one.

prep time:
10 minutes

cook time:
20 minutes

½ cup nondairy milk

1 tbsp white vinegar

1 cup gluten-free all-purpose flour

½ cup almond flour

½ cup coconut sugar

2 tsp baking powder

1 tsp baking soda

2 tsp ground cinnamon

⅓ cup macadamia oil or olive oil

2 tbsp maple syrup

1 tsp pure vanilla extract

½ cup chopped walnuts

¼ cup raisins

¼ cup shredded coconut

1. Preheat the oven to 400°F (200°C). Line 12 cups of a muffin pan with paper liners. (Or grease with macadamia, olive, or coconut oil.)

2. In a small bowl, combine the nondairy milk and vinegar to make vegan buttermilk.

3. In a large bowl, combine the flour, almond flour, coconut sugar, baking powder, baking soda, and cinnamon. Mix together.

4. Stir in the macadamia oil, maple syrup, and vanilla, along with the buttermilk mixture. Mix until combined. Fold in the walnuts, raisins, and coconut.

5. Scoop the mixture into the prepared muffin pan.

6. Bake for 20 minutes or until the tops are firm and a toothpick comes out clean. Let them cool for 15 minutes. Store in an airtight container for up to 3 days on the counter.

chickpea frittata egg muffins

SERVES 12

Did you know you can make plant-based egg muffins using chickpea flour? It's one of the best healthy vegan hacks out there. Make a batch for the week, then keep in the fridge and reheat for grab-and-go breakfasts, or for something to snack on throughout the day.

prep time:
10 minutes

cook time:
35 minutes

1 cup peeled and diced russet potato

½ cup diced white onion

1 cup diced red bell pepper

1 tbsp olive oil

1¾ cups chickpea flour

¼ cup nutritional yeast

1 tsp baking powder

1 tsp garlic powder

1 tsp salt

¼ tsp pepper

½ tsp ground turmeric

½ tsp smoked paprika

2 cups unsweetened almond milk

1–2 cups chopped spinach

¼ cup minced fresh chives

1. Preheat the oven to 375°F (190°C). Lightly grease a 12-cup muffin pan with olive or avocado oil, or line with paper liners.

2. In a microwave-safe bowl, combine the potato, onion, and bell pepper. Add the olive oil and microwave on high for 4 minutes to soften.

3. In a large bowl, whisk together the chickpea flour, nutritional yeast, baking powder, garlic powder, salt, pepper, turmeric, and smoked paprika. Stir in the milk. Add the spinach and mix again.

4. Using a ¼-cup measure, scoop the mixture into the prepared muffin pan. Sprinkle the chives evenly over the muffins.

5. Bake for 35 to 45 minutes or until muffins are set and golden brown at the edges.

6. Enjoy immediately or refrigerate for up to 4 days—perfect for a snack, or breakfast on-the-go for work or school.

HealthyGirl Tip

If you want some alternative veggie options, I recommend zucchini, sweet potato, mushrooms, or kale—any of these would be great!

girl-on-the-go breakfast burrito

SERVES 1

Where are my savory girls at? This plant-based breakfast burrito is high in protein, which means it keeps you full longer and is the *perfect* post-workout meal. Go to a Pilates class or take a long walk with your BFF, then make these burritos after. I promise you won't regret it.

prep time:
5 minutes

cook time:
10 minutes

1 large (10-inch) tortilla

4 oz extra-firm tofu, squeezed dry and crumbled

1 tbsp almond milk

½ tsp ground turmeric

¼ tsp garlic powder

Salt and pepper, to taste

½ cup fresh spinach, lightly packed

¼ cup canned black beans, rinsed and drained

½ avocado, sliced

½ tomato, sliced

1–2 tbsp salsa

1. Lay the tortilla flat on a cutting board.

2. In a nonstick pan over medium heat, sauté the crumbled tofu with the almond milk, turmeric, garlic powder, and a pinch of salt and pepper until heated through. Add to the center of the tortilla.

3. In the same pan over medium heat, sauté the spinach for 60 seconds. Layer the spinach atop the tofu.

4. Add the black beans, avocado slices, tomato slices, and salsa to the tortilla. Roll up tightly.

5. In the same pan over medium heat, crisp the burrito to seal the tortilla, turning once, until golden brown.

6. Cut in half and dig in, or roll in foil and eat on the go!

HealthyGirl Tip

Meal prep a big batch of tofu scramble to keep in the fridge as well as a container of rinsed and drained black beans to make super-quick breakfast burritos. Use the full block of tofu and triple the spices to make a bigger batch of the scramble.

healthygirl salads + bowls

fall in love with nourishing your body

kale caesar salad

SERVES 4

This kale Caesar salad is going to be your new obsession. The crisp lettuce, creamy dressing, and crunchy homemade croutons will have you making this on repeat. If you previously didn't like kale, this salad will change your mind. Make this to go with dinner, for your friends when they come over, or to bring to a party.

prep time:
15 minutes

cook time:
10 minutes

2 slices of sourdough bread, cut into croutons

Olive oil spray

Salt and pepper, to taste

3 cups chopped dinosaur (lacinato) kale

1 head romaine, chopped

Must-Have Cashew Caesar Dressing (page 72)

Vegan parmesan:
¾ cup almonds

3 tbsp nutritional yeast

¾ tsp salt

¼ tsp garlic powder

1. Preheat the oven to 425°F (220°C). Line a baking sheet with parchment paper.

2. Spread the croutons out onto the prepared baking sheet. Coat with olive oil spray and season with salt and pepper.

3. Bake the croutons for 10 minutes, tossing once, until golden brown.

4. In a food processor, blend the vegan parmesan ingredients until they're completely combined. It will look like parm!

5. In a large bowl, combine the kale and romaine. Toss with Must-Have Cashew Caesar Dressing to taste.

6. Sprinkle the croutons on top, and add as much vegan parmesan as you want. (Save the rest in a sealed jar in the fridge.)

glowing skin salad

SERVES 4

Lentils are one of those legumes that are truly a superfood. They have the highest protein content of any bean, packing in 18 grams per cup. Lentils are also very high in fiber and have about 16 grams per cup. Aside from being a protein and fiber powerhouse, lentils are a great source of iron, folate, and B vitamins. The beets, tomatoes, and parsley are great for skin health. The moral of the story is simple: eat more lentils.

prep time:
20 minutes

2 cups French lentils, rinsed well

1 cup steamed and quartered beets

1 cup diced yellow tomatoes

½ cup chopped fresh parsley

1 orange (optional), peeled and sliced

½ cup thinly sliced red onion

¾ cup shelled pistachios

Citrus Vinaigrette (page 74)

Salt and pepper, to taste

Arugula, for serving

1. Bring a medium pot of water to a boil. Add the lentils and cook for 15 to 20 minutes, or until tender (not mushy). Drain and add to a large bowl.

2. Add the beets, tomatoes, parsley, orange (if using), onion, and pistachios to the lentils.

3. Toss with Citrus Vinaigrette, season to taste with salt and pepper, serve on a bed of arugula, and enjoy! Store the lentil salad in the fridge for up to 3 days.

> **HealthyGirl Tip**
> Adding this salad to a bed of arugula is a total game changer, and you'll get your greens in for the day!

summer corn + avocado salad

SERVES 3–4

This is the absolute perfect addition to any summer party. Did you know corn is rich in vitamin C? The fresh corn, sweet mango, creamy avocado, and crunchy pepper mixed together reminds me of summer happiness. Whenever I make this for someone, they always ask me for the recipe.

prep time:
10 minutes

cook time:
5 minutes

3 cups corn

1 cup diced mango

1 avocado, diced

1 cup diced bell pepper

¼ cup finely diced red onion

Creamy Cilantro Dressing (page 74)

Salt and pepper, to taste

1. Cut the corn off the cobs, add into a large microwave-safe bowl, and cook for 3 minutes. Let it cool for 5 to 10 minutes.

2. In a bowl, add the corn, mango, avocado, bell pepper, and red onion.

3. Toss with Creamy Cilantro Dressing, season to taste with salt and pepper, and enjoy!

HealthyGirl Tip

Pair with a big handful of fresh tortilla chips for a delightfully crunchy combination!

fall harvest salad

SERVES 2–3

When I made a bowl of this for my mother-in-law, she said it was "the perfect salad." I would have to agree. It's the perfect balance of sweetness from the figs, pomegranate seeds, apple, and cranberries, paired with savory and salty flavors from the Brussels sprouts, kale, and pecans. This salad will instantly remind you of fall because of its warm colors and vibrant flavors.

prep time:
15 minutes

cook time:
10 minutes

1 cup peeled, cubed sweet potato

Olive oil spray

1 tsp ground cinnamon

Salt and pepper, to taste

4 cups shredded kale

1 cup shredded Brussels sprouts

1 apple, diced

½ cup chopped dried figs

½ cup chopped pecans

Basic Balsamic Vinaigrette (page 75)

½ cup pomegranate seeds

½ cup dried cranberries

1. Preheat the oven to 450°F (230°C), and line a baking sheet with parchment paper.

2. Coat the sweet potato cubes with olive oil spray, and season with the cinnamon, salt, and pepper. Roast for about 10 minutes

3. In a large bowl, combine the kale, Brussels sprouts, apple, figs, pecans, and roasted sweet potato.

4. Toss with Basic Balsamic Vinaigrette to taste.

5. Top with the pomegranate seeds and dried cranberries, and serve.

> **HealthyGirl Tip**
> For a quick method, spray 1 cup peeled and cubed sweet potato with olive oil, season with salt and pepper, and microwave for 5 minutes in a microwave-safe bowl.

taco salad

SERVES 4

This is the kind of salad you want to shovel into your mouth. It's basically all of your favorite taco ingredients chopped up in a bowl. If you need a healthy and easy light lunch to bring to work or school, this salad is perfect! Just keep the dressing and tortilla strips on the side so they don't get soggy.

prep time:
10 minutes

cook time:
10 minutes

2 whole-grain tortillas, sliced into strips

Olive oil spray

Salt, to taste

2 cups corn kernels (from about 2 ears or frozen)

1 head romaine lettuce, chopped

½ cup chopped cilantro

1 (15 oz) can black beans, rinsed and drained

1 cup diced tomatoes

1 avocado, cubed

Southwest Dressing (page 75)

1. Preheat the oven to 425°F (220°C). Line a baking sheet with parchment paper.

2. Spread the tortilla strips on the baking sheet. Coat with olive oil spray and season with salt. Bake for 8 minutes, tossing once, until golden brown and crispy.

3. Meanwhile, microwave the corn in a microwave-safe bowl for about 3 minutes. Set aside to cool slightly.

4. In a large bowl, combine the romaine lettuce, cilantro, black beans, tomatoes, avocado, and corn.

5. Top the salad with tortilla strips and toss with Southwest Dressing to taste.

gf sf nf 20

bbq chickpea chopped salad

SERVES 4–5

My mom has always called me a drama queen, but I swear I'm not being dramatic when I say this is one of the top three best salads I've ever had. You know how restaurant salads tend to taste better than the ones you make at home? This salad changed that for me. When I first made it, my husband immediately said, "This tastes like a restaurant salad." It's smoky, sweet, crunchy, creamy, and crispy. This will be your new favorite salad.

prep time:
10 minutes

cook time:
5 minutes

1 (15 oz) can chickpeas, rinsed and drained

½ cup BBQ sauce

1½ heads romaine lettuce, chopped

1½ cups halved cherry tomatoes

1 cup freshly steamed corn

1 avocado, cubed

½ cup chopped cilantro

2 handfuls crushed corn chips

¼ cup diced red onion

Hempseed Ranch Dressing (page 76)

1. In a saucepan over medium heat, sauté the chickpeas in the BBQ sauce for about 5 minutes, until the sauce has thickened and the chickpeas are heated through.

2. In a large bowl, combine the romaine lettuce, tomatoes, corn, avocado, cilantro, crushed chips, and red onion.

3. Toss with Hempseed Ranch Dressing to taste, top with the chickpeas, and enjoy!

gf sf lf

mediterranean pesto quinoa salad

SERVES 4

You might have put pesto on pasta, but have you ever added it to quinoa?
Let me tell ya, it's beyond yummy. Quinoa is not a grain; it's actually a seed.
It's gluten-free, and packed with magnesium, potassium, fiber, and protein.
It's much more nutrient dense than rice, so this is your sign to eat more
meals with quinoa. Serving quinoa with arugula is a good chance to add
more greens to your diet (which we all know we need more of).

prep time:
10 minutes

cook time:
15 minutes

1 cup quinoa

2 cups water

½ cup pine nuts

Plant-Based Pesto Please (page 76)

½ cup chopped oil-packed or dry sun-dried tomatoes

Arugula

½ lemon

1. To a medium pot, add the quinoa and water. Bring to a boil, then cover and reduce to a simmer. Cook for 10 to 15 minutes, until all the water is absorbed, then fluff with a fork.

2. In a saucepan, toast the pine nuts over medium heat, stirring constantly until golden brown.

3. Add the Plant-Based Pesto Please to the cooked quinoa, along with the pine nuts and sun-dried tomatoes, and mix gently.

4. Serve on top of a bed of arugula for extra green goodness.

5. Squeeze the lemon juice over top to taste and enjoy! Store any extra pesto quinoa in the fridge for up to 5 days.

sf nf lf 20

greek pasta salad

SERVES 6

I could eat this every single day. Anything pasta-related is my favorite food, but this Greek-inspired pasta salad is not only super simple to make, it's also fresh, light, and yummy. Make a big batch at the beginning of the week for easy lunches, to bring to a potluck, or to serve with the Lemon Caper Tofu Filets (page 160) for the best dinner.

prep time:
10 minutes

6 oz rotini, cooked and cooled slightly

1 (15 oz) can chickpeas, rinsed and drained

½ cup pitted and sliced kalamata olives

1 cup halved cherry tomatoes

1 cup diced cucumber

½ cup diced red onion

Greek Girl Dressing (page 77)

½ cup vegan feta, crumbled (optional)

1. In a large bowl, combine the pasta, chickpeas, olives, tomatoes, cucumber, and red onion.

2. Toss with Greek Girl Dressing to taste.

3. Top with crumbled vegan feta (if using) and enjoy!

HealthyGirl Tip
You can keep this pasta salad in the fridge for up to 4 days.

protein power bowl

SERVES 1

This is one of those bowls you will crave all the time because of how good it makes you feel. It's my go-to lunch because it's so easy to make, and keeps me satiated for hours. This is one of those super-simple, plant-based meals that has numerous health benefits. Add chickpeas to more of your meals because the longest living populations are bean eaters!

prep time:
10 minutes

cook time:
15 minutes

1 cup cubed high-protein, extra-firm tofu

Olive oil

Salt and pepper, to taste

1 tsp garlic powder

2 tbsp coconut aminos

1 cup fresh spinach

½ cup cooked rice or quinoa

½ cup chickpeas, rinsed and drained

4 tomato slices

Maple Dijon Tahini Dressing (page 77)

Optional toppings:

Carrots

Pumpkin seeds

Red Cabbage

1. In a pan over medium heat, sauté the tofu in olive oil, and season with salt, pepper, and garlic powder.

2. Once crispy, add the coconut aminos and sauté for another two minutes until the coconut aminos thicken.

3. In a salad bowl, add the spinach, cooked tofu, rice, chickpeas, and tomato slices.

4. Toss with Maple Dijon Tahini Dressing to taste.

green goddess bowl

SERVES 1

This is one of the most-made meals in our household. If you're someone who struggles to eat enough veggies, this bowl is the best solution. I've found that the key to eating more veggies is to pair them with pasta and a yummy sauce (like pesto). Of course, I created this bowl to be perfectly balanced with complex carbs from the whole-grain pasta; protein and fiber from the beans; more fiber from the veggies; and healthy fats from the hempseed, avocado, and pesto.

prep time:
15 minutes

cook time:
15 minutes

Olive oil

½ cup diced zucchini

1 cup chopped kale

½ cup asparagus, cut in 1-inch pieces

1 cup cooked whole-grain or gluten-free pasta

½ cup white beans, rinsed and drained

½ avocado, cubed

1 batch **Plant-Based Pesto Please** (page 76)

1 tbsp hempseed

1 lemon, sliced, for garnish

1. Heat olive oil in a sauté pan over medium heat. Sauté the zucchini, kale, and asparagus until crisp-tender.

2. Add the pasta, beans, sautéed veggies, and avocado to a large bowl. Toss with the Plant-Based Pesto Please to taste.

3. Sprinkle with hempseed, and garnish with lemon.

healthygirl dressings

sauces, dips, and dressings to pour on everything

must-have cashew caesar dressing

Caesar salad dressing is traditionally made with eggs and anchovies. It's salty, garlicky, and so freaking yummy. Being the caesar salad addict that I am, when I started a plant-based diet, I knew I had to create the best vegan caesar dressing. You're welcome.

prep time:
5 minutes

1 cup raw cashews

1 tbsp olive oil

2 tbsp lemon juice

1 tbsp capers

1 tbsp caper brine

2 tsp Dijon mustard

½ tsp salt

¾ cup water

1 tsp garlic powder

Pinch of pepper

1. Blend all the ingredients together in a blender until completely smooth.

2. Store in the fridge in an airtight jar, bottle, or container for up to 5 days. Pairs perfectly with the **Kale Caesar Salad** (page 50).

HealthyGirl Tip

If you don't have a high-speed blender like a Vitamix, boil the cashews for 5 minutes to soften, then rinse with cold water before blending.

citrus vinaigrette

This citrus vinaigrette is the perfect balance of acidic, sweet, and savory. It pairs perfectly with quinoa salad, lentil salad, or even kale salad. Adding orange juice to dressings is a great way to add extra vitamin C and vitamin A.

prep time:
5 minutes

½ cup olive oil

3 tbsp white wine vinegar

2 tbsp fresh orange juice

1 tbsp lemon juice

1 tbsp maple syrup

½ tsp garlic powder

½ tsp salt

Pinch of pepper

1. Whisk all the ingredients together in a bowl, or blend in a blender until well combined.

2. Store in the fridge in an airtight jar, bottle, or container for up to 5 days. Pairs perfectly with the **Glowing Skin Salad** (page 53).

HealthyGirl Tip

Instead of whisking, you can also try putting all the ingredients in a jar and giving it a good shake: super easy, and fewer dishes to wash as you can store the leftovers in the same jar.

---

creamy cilantro dressing

This creamy cilantro dressing gets its creaminess from cashews. You don't need dairy to make a delicious, creamy dressing. You can pair this dressing with a salad or even make it as a taco topping or a great dip for veggies! This dressing is packed with cilantro, which is great for improving heart health and brain health, and boosting energy levels.

prep time:
5 minutes

¼ cup olive oil

¼ cup water

½ cup cashews

1 tbsp lime juice

1 cup cilantro

½ tsp salt

¼ tsp pepper

Pinch of cayenne pepper

1. Blend all the ingredients together in a blender until completely smooth.

2. Store in the fridge in an airtight jar, bottle, or container for up to 5 days. Pairs perfectly with the **Summer Corn + Avocado Salad** (page 54).

HealthyGirl Tip

If you don't have a high-speed blender like a Vitamix, boil the cashews for 5 to 10 minutes, then rinse with cold water.

basic balsamic vinaigrette

Every girl needs to know how to make a balsamic vinaigrette, and this one is perfect. This is my most-made dressing because I always have the ingredients on hand, and you probably do too. I recommend keeping balsamic and oil stocked in your home at all times; they are pantry staples.

prep time:
5 minutes

¼ cup olive oil

3 tbsp balsamic vinegar

1 tsp Dijon mustard

1 clove garlic, minced (optional)

Salt and pepper, to taste

1. Whisk all the ingredients together in a bowl until well combined.

2. Store in the fridge in an airtight jar, bottle, or container for up to 2 weeks. Pairs perfectly with the **Fall Harvest Salad** (page 57).

southwest dressing

This creamy Southwest Dressing is made with yogurt. Using yogurt to make creamy dressings is one of my favorite healthy tips. Yogurt is filled with probiotics, and it's great for the gut. It's also less calorie dense and more heart healthy than real mayonnaise.

prep time:
5 minutes

1 cup plain vegan yogurt

2 tbsp olive oil

1 tbsp maple syrup

¼ cup lime juice

2 tsp chili powder

1 tsp smoked paprika

½ tsp garlic

½ tsp onion powder

½ tsp ground cumin

¼ tsp salt

Pinch of pepper

1. Whisk all the ingredients together in a bowl until well combined.

2. Store in the fridge in an airtight jar, bottle, or container for up to 4 days. Pairs perfectly with the **Taco Salad** (page 58).

hempseed ranch dressing

This is the healthiest version of plant-based ranch dressing you'll find. If you're like me and could smother everything in ranch dressing, you need to make this hempseed ranch. It's creamy; packed with healthy fats, fiber, and protein from the hempseed; and whips up in the blender in less than a few minutes. Use this as a dressing for pasta salad or a fresh, green salad, or as a dip for veggies like cucumbers and peppers, or even for plant-based chicken tenders.

prep time:
5 minutes

¾ cup hempseed

¾ cup water

2 tbsp olive oil

Juice from 1 lemon

1 tsp garlic powder

1 tsp dried parsley

2 tsp dried dill

1 tsp apple cider vinegar

1 tsp salt

1. Blend all the ingredients together in a blender until completely smooth.

2. Store in the fridge in an airtight jar, bottle, or container for up to 5 days. Pairs perfectly with the **BBQ Chickpea Chopped Salad** (page 61).

plant-based pesto please

If you're a pesto lover, stop right here. This is going to be your new go-to pesto. To make this dairy-free, you actually use nutritional yeast instead of Parmesan cheese. It gives the pesto that cheesy flavor and also packs it with B vitamins. Add this pesto to bowls, salads, pasta dishes, and even over top of tofu.

prep time:
5 minutes

2 cups fresh basil

2 cups fresh spinach

½ cup olive oil

½ cup raw cashews

1 tbsp lemon juice

¼ cup nutritional yeast

1–2 cloves garlic or 1 tsp garlic powder

½ tsp pink salt, or more to taste

1. Blend all the ingredients together in a food processor until well combined.

2. Store in the fridge in an airtight jar, bottle, or container for up to 5 days. Pairs perfectly with the **Mediterranean Pesto Quinoa Salad** (page 62).

greek girl dressing

If any of the HealthyGirl dressing recipes are going to be on repeat in your house, it's going to be this Greek Girl Dressing. It's not only yummy when added to pasta salads but also delicious when served on a fresh, green salad, or even served over warm grilled veggies.

prep time:
5 minutes

½ cup olive oil

3 tbsp red wine vinegar

1 tbsp lemon juice

1 tsp Dijon mustard

1 tsp dried oregano

1 tsp garlic powder

½ tsp salt

¼ tsp pepper

1. Whisk all the ingredients together in a bowl, or shake in a jar.

2. Store in the fridge in an airtight jar, bottle, or container for up to 5 days. Pairs perfectly with the **Greek Pasta Salad** (page 65).

maple dijon tahini dressing

This creamy tahini dressing is good enough to drink. Tahini—made from ground sesame seeds—makes the dressing creamy without the dairy. Keep tahini on hand because it's a pantry staple and it's packed with healthy fats.

prep time:
5 minutes

¼ cup tahini

1 tbsp maple syrup

1 tsp Dijon mustard

3 tbsp lemon juice

2 tbsp water

1. Whisk all the ingredients together in a bowl until well combined.

2. Store in the fridge in an airtight jar, bottle, or container for up to 10 days. Pairs perfectly with the **Protein Power Bowl** (page 66).

sesame peanut dressing

This dressing is so good and so versatile. It's delicious paired with Asian noodle dishes or chopped salads, or even used as a dip for wraps.

prep time:
5 minutes

½ cup peanut butter

1 tbsp sriracha

4 tbsp soy sauce or coconut aminos

1 tbsp lime juice

3 tbsp rice vinegar

¼ cup water

1 tbsp maple syrup

1 tbsp toasted sesame oil

1 tsp garlic powder

1½ tsp ground ginger

1. Mix all the ingredients together in a bowl until completely smooth.

2. Store in the fridge in an airtight jar, bottle, or container for up to 7 days. Pairs perfectly with the **Rainbow Peanut Noodles** (page 172).

antioxidant blueberry dressing

Blueberries are one of those superfoods that should always be in your fridge. They are one of the most nutrient-dense berries and are a great source of gut-friendly fiber, vitamin C, potassium, and manganese, and have some of the highest antioxidant content when compared to other fruits and veggies. Eat more blueberries, starting with this delicious, vibrant dressing.

**prep time:
5 minutes**

2 cups blueberries

⅓ cup olive oil

¼ cup balsamic vinegar

1 tbsp maple syrup

2 tsp Dijon mustard

Salt and pepper, to taste

1. Blend all the ingredients together in a blender until completely smooth.

2. Store in the fridge in an airtight jar, bottle, or container for up to 3 days.

> **HealthyGirl Tip**
> Be sure to give the dressing a good shake before using it after storing it in the fridge!

healthygirl soups

because gorgeous girls love soup

20-minute minestrone soup

SERVES 8

I swear minestrone soup nourishes the soul. My go-to appetizer order at Italian restaurants while growing up was, without fail, a cup of minestrone soup. The second there's a slight chill in the air, I make a big batch of this plant-based minestrone soup. It's packed with veggies and beans, which promote longevity. There's nothing quite like a bowl of this soup paired with some crusty sourdough bread.

prep time:
5 minutes

cook time:
15 minutes

2 tbsp olive oil

1 cup diced onion

½ cup diced celery

½ cup diced carrots

1 cup chopped green beans (fresh or frozen)

1 (15 oz) can cannellini beans, rinsed and drained

4 cups veggie broth

1 (15 oz) can diced tomatoes

1 tsp dried oregano

1 tsp dried basil

1 tsp salt

¼ tsp pepper

2 cups cooked ditalini pasta

Vegan parmesan (optional)

1. In a large soup pot, heat the olive oil over medium heat. Add the onion, celery, and carrots. Sauté for 5 minutes.

2. Add the green beans and cannellini beans into the pot and stir.

3. Pour in the veggie broth, and add the full can of diced tomatoes as well. Add the oregano, basil, salt, and pepper, and stir.

4. Bring to a boil, then let simmer for 10 minutes.

5. Add the pasta into the pot and stir. Top with vegan parmesan (if using) and enjoy!

6. Store in the fridge for up to 4 days. If you want to prevent the noodles from getting mushy, keep them separate in the fridge and add them to the soup when reheating for leftovers.

anti-inflammatory lentil soup

SERVES 6

Lentils are high in fiber and phytonutrients, which both help fight inflammation. This soup also has turmeric and antioxidant-rich kale, which combat inflammation as well. Moral of the story is: this soup is incredible for your health, but is also super warming, healing, and cozy. This is the best snuggle-up-on-your-couch-with-a-blanket kind of soup there is.

prep time:
10 minutes

cook time:
40 minutes

1 cup diced yellow onion

2 tsp minced garlic

1 cup diced carrots

1 cup diced celery

½ tsp ground cumin

½ tsp turmeric

1 tsp coriander

1 tbsp olive oil

1½ cups green lentils, rinsed

10 cups veggie broth

1 tsp salt

¼ cup chopped fresh parsley, divided

¼ cup chopped fresh dill, divided

2 cups chopped kale

1 tbsp lemon juice

¼ tsp pepper

1. In a large soup pot, sauté the onion, garlic, carrots, celery, cumin, turmeric, and coriander in olive oil over medium heat for 3 minutes.

2. Into the pot, add the lentils, veggie broth, salt, parsley, and dill. Save 1 tablespoon of the parsley and dill to use later.

3. Bring to a boil, then partially cover and cook for 30 minutes until the lentils are tender.

4. Add the kale, lemon juice, and pepper, and cook for another 5 minutes, or until the kale is tender. Top with the reserved parsley and dill.

5. Store in the fridge for up to 5 days.

gf sf lf

creamy broccoli cheddar soup

SERVES 6

This broccoli cheddar soup is honestly the best excuse to eat something out of a bread bowl. I used to be such a Panera girl—in high school, I'd study there with my friends and we'd always get salad and soup in a bread bowl. This recipe is 100 percent Panera inspired, and it doesn't disappoint.

prep time:
5 minutes

cook time:
20 minutes

2 large russet potatoes, peeled and quartered

2 medium carrots, roughly chopped

½ cup raw cashews

1 cup diced yellow onion

1 (16 oz) bag frozen broccoli (or 4 cups cut-up fresh broccoli)

1 tbsp olive oil

½ cup nutritional yeast

1 tsp garlic powder

1 tsp salt

½ tsp dry mustard

½ tsp pepper

1 cup unsweetened nondairy milk

2 cups veggie broth

¼ tsp turmeric

1. In a large pot, boil the potatoes, carrots, and cashews and cook until soft. Strain and add into a blender.

2. In a large soup pot, sauté the onion and broccoli in olive oil over medium-high heat until cooked and the broccoli is easily broken up with a spatula.

3. Into the blender with the cashews, carrots, and potatoes, add the nutritional yeast, garlic powder, salt, dry mustard, pepper, nondairy milk, and veggie broth. Blend until completely smooth. Add water, ¼ cup at a time, if you want it to be thinner.

4. Pour the potato-cheese mixture into the soup pot with the broccoli. Add the turmeric. Heat on medium until warmed all the way through.

sheet pan tomato + zucchini soup

SERVES 4

This is about to be the best tomato soup you'll ever have. Roasting the tomatoes makes them that much more flavorful. The secret to sneaking more veggies into this soup is adding a whole zucchini. I recommend making a few batches of this, freezing it, and keeping it for the colder months. Thaw the soup and heat it when you're ready to eat it. Pair it with a vegan grilled cheese or a fresh baguette.

prep time:
5 minutes

cook time:
40 minutes

10 Roma tomatoes, halved

1 large zucchini, cut into rounds

1 red onion, roughly chopped

3 cloves garlic, peeled

2 tbsp olive oil, plus more for serving

1 tsp salt

½ tsp pepper

3 sprigs fresh thyme, plus more for serving

½ cup full-fat coconut milk

Garnish:

Croutons (optional)

Fresh lemon wedges

Fresh cracked black pepper

1. Preheat the oven to 400°F (200°C).

2. Line a baking sheet with parchment paper.

3. Place the tomatoes, zucchini, onion, and garlic cloves onto the prepared baking sheet.

4. Drizzle on the olive oil, and season with the salt and pepper.

5. Place the whole sprigs of fresh thyme on top of the veggies.

6. Roast for 40 minutes.

7. Remove the thyme from the stem and sprinkle on top of the roasted veggies. Scoop the roasted veggies and any liquid in the pan into a blender.

8. Pour the coconut milk into the blender, and blend until creamy and smooth.

9. Top with croutons, if using, a squeeze of fresh lemon, a crack of black pepper, a drizzle of olive oil, and more fresh thyme.

corn + sweet potato chili

SERVES 5

You know what I've realized? Everyone likes chili. If there's one healthy meal you need to know how to make, it's vegan chili. It's warm, hearty, and filling, and meat-eaters beg for the recipe. This chili hits the spot every single time. Oh, and be sure to serve it with cornbread . . . you're welcome.

prep time:
10 minutes

cook time:
20 minutes

Chili:

1 tbsp olive oil

½ yellow onion, diced

1 yellow bell pepper, diced

1 red bell pepper, diced

1 tsp salt

¼ tsp pepper

1 tsp chili powder

½ tsp ground cumin

½ tsp garlic powder

½ tsp smoked paprika

1 medium sweet potato, peeled and cubed

1 (15 oz) can black beans, rinsed and drained

1 (15 oz) can kidney beans, rinsed and drained

1 (15 oz) can great northern beans, rinsed and drained

1 cup corn, cut off the cob or frozen

1 (15 oz) can tomato sauce

1 (15 oz) can diced tomatoes

1½ cups water

Cornbread (optional), for serving

Fresh lime wedges, for serving

Cashew sour cream:

1½ cups raw cashews (microwave in a bowl with water for 5 minutes to soften)

1 tsp apple cider vinegar

2 tbsp lemon juice

1 cup water

1. Heat a large soup pot to medium on the stove top.

2. Once heated, add the olive oil, onion, yellow bell pepper, red bell pepper, salt, and pepper. Sauté for 5 minutes.

3. Add the chili powder, cumin, garlic powder, and paprika. Cook for 1 minute more.

4. Add the sweet potato, beans, corn, tomato sauce, diced tomatoes, and water.

5. Bring to a boil then reduce heat to low, cover, and simmer for 15 minutes.

6. While the chili cooks, make the sour cream by adding all the ingredients to a blender. Blend until completely smooth. If the cashew sauce isn't blending completely, add more water, 2 tablespoons at a time until smooth.

7. Serve with toppings like vegan sour cream, cilantro, red onion, and even cornbread! A squeeze of fresh lime juice on top and a little hot sauce makes this even more flavorful.

gut-friendly butternut squash soup

SERVES 4

If you're bloated and need an easy-to-digest meal, this butternut squash soup is very gentle on the stomach. Butternut squash is one of those foods that you need to keep around because its vitamins and fiber content work to improve gut health. In the colder months, make sure to have this soup on hand for a quick, warm meal.

prep time:
10 minutes

cook time:
25 minutes

2 tbsp olive oil

¾ cup diced yellow onion

4–6 cloves garlic, finely minced

1 tsp salt

¼ tsp pepper

2 lb frozen or fresh butternut squash, cubed

4 cups veggie broth

¼ tsp ground ginger

¼ tsp nutmeg

1 (14 oz) can full-fat coconut milk

1 tbsp maple syrup

1. Heat a large soup pot to medium on the stove top. Once heated, add the olive oil, onion, garlic, salt, and pepper. Sauté until translucent.

2. Add the butternut squash, and sauté for another 10 minutes.

3. Pour in the veggie broth, and add the ginger, and nutmeg.

4. Bring to a boil, then simmer for 10 minutes, stirring frequently.

5. Add the coconut milk into the pot, then pour the mixture into the blender and blend until completely smooth.

6. Add the soup back into the pot to reheat it. Add the maple syrup. Once fully heated, serve and enjoy!

> **HealthyGirl Tip**
> If you don't have a large, high-speed blender, you will need to puree this soup in batches. An immersion blender can also be used directly in the pot.

"get well" lemon rice soup

SERVES 4

Feeling under the weather? Make this healing, warm, clear broth lemon rice soup to comfort you on your sick days. Of course you can make this even if you're not sick, but it's especially soothing when you're congested and stuffy. The lemon adds vitamin C and a freshness to the soup that's so delicious.

prep time:
5 minutes

cook time:
35 minutes

2 tbsp olive oil

1 cup diced white onion

1½ cups diced carrots, (about 3 carrots)

3 stalks celery, chopped

1 tsp salt

2 bay leaves

4 cups veggie broth

½ cup short-grain brown rice

1 cup water

¼ tsp pepper

¼ cup lemon juice

½ cup chopped fresh parsley

1. Heat a large soup pot to medium on the stove top. Add the olive oil, onion, carrots, and celery.

2. Add the salt and sauté for 5 minutes. Then add the bay leaves, veggie broth, brown rice, and water.

3. Bring to a boil, then cover and reduce to a simmer. Cook for 30 minutes, or until the rice is tender. Remove the bay leaves.

4. Add the pepper, lemon juice, and parsley.

HealthyGirl Tip
Serve with crackers or some really good bread.

---

vegan french onion soup

SERVES 2

French onion soup is a classic. It's cozy, rich, robust, and flavorful. Let's be honest, the best part of French onion soup is the bread in the middle that has soaked up all the yummy broth. If you can find vegan mozzarella in your local grocery store to melt on top of the bread, it makes this delicious recipe even better.

prep time:
5 minutes

cook time:
45 minutes

2 tbsp olive oil

4 large yellow onions, thinly sliced

1 tsp dried thyme

1 tsp salt

½ tsp pepper

1 tbsp flour

½ cup white wine

4 cups veggie broth

1 bay leaf

1 tbsp balsamic vinegar

1 baguette

Vegan mozzarella (optional)

1. Add the olive oil to a large soup pot, and add the onion, thyme, salt, and pepper.

2. Sauté for 20 to 25 minutes on medium-low heat, stirring occasionally, until the onions are caramelized and golden.

3. Sprinkle in the flour, and mix until well combined. Cook for a minute.

4. Pour in the wine, stirring to scrape up any brown bits at the bottom of the pot, and cook for a few minutes until the wine is reduced.

5. Add the veggie broth and bay leaf. Bring to a boil, then simmer for 20 minutes. Remove the bay leaf.

6. Add the balsamic vinegar once the soup is done simmering.

7. Slice the baguette, and toast each slice in the oven or in a toaster. Add a slice to each bowl of soup.

HealthyGirl Tip

If you're able to find vegan mozzarella cheese in your local store, melt it on top of the crostini in the oven by broiling until the cheese is melted.

5-minute miso soup

SERVES 4

Sushi night isn't complete without miso soup. I used to think miso soup was something I needed to order in a restaurant because it'd be too complicated to make. I was wrong! It literally takes five minutes. Miso has some great health benefits: it's packed with zinc, potassium, and calcium. Miso is also great for gut health and boosting the immune system.

prep time:
3 minutes

cook time:
5 minutes

4 cups veggie broth

¼ cup white miso paste

1 cup chopped kale

3 tbsp wakame

1 tbsp soy sauce

½ block silken tofu, cubed

Scallions for garnish

1. In a large soup pot, bring the veggie broth to a low boil.

2. In a small bowl, combine the miso paste and about ½ cup of hot broth, and whisk to dissolve. Set aside.

3. Into the pot, stir the kale, wakame, and soy sauce, and cook for 3 minutes.

4. Reduce the heat to low, stir in the tofu and reserved miso mixture, and continue to cook just until the tofu is heated through, about 1 minute.

5. Garnish with scallions and serve.

green detox soup

SERVES 4

This soup is packed with disease-fighting, antioxidant-rich, green veggies. Broccoli and kale are extremely nutrient-dense cruciferous veggies, which contain glucosinolates. Glucosinolates can help fight bacterial, fungal, and viral infections. Not to mention, this vibrant soup has an abundance of dietary fiber, which will prevent constipation and improve gut health. I specifically added parsley to this soup for liver support.

prep time:
15 minutes

cook time:
15 minutes

1 cup diced yellow onion

1 cup sliced leeks

1 tsp salt

1 tbsp olive oil

2 parsnips, chopped

2 cups broccoli florets

2 cups fresh spinach

1 cup chopped kale

½ cup fresh parsley

2 tbsp hempseed

½ cup full-fat coconut milk

1 cup veggie broth, or mote to taste

¼ tsp pepper

1 tsp lemon juice

1. In a large soup pot, add the onion, leeks, and salt, and sauté in the olive oil for a few minutes on medium heat.

2. Add the parsnips, broccoli, spinach, kale, and parsley. Sauté for 10 to 15 minutes or until tender and cooked.

3. Scoop the cooked veggies into a blender. Also add the hempseed, coconut milk, veggie broth, pepper, and lemon juice.

4. Blend until completely smooth, then pour back into the pot. If you don't have a big blender, blend the soup in a few batches or use an immersion blender directly in the pot.

5. Add 1 more cup of veggie broth if you'd like the soup to be thinner. Heat until warmed.

> **HealthyGirl Tip**
> Cut the dark green tops off the leeks as well as the root. Cut the white part lengthwise then cut into thin, half-circle pieces. Rinse in water to get any dirt off.

healthygirl sandwiches

veggie wraps + sandwiches you'll crave

california girl veggie sandwich

SERVES 1

If you need a go-to, meat-free sandwich, this veggie-packed California girl sandwich will show you that you don't need deli meat and cheese to make a great sammie. The creamy avocado, crunchy cucumbers, crispy lettuce, spicy mustard, and fresh sprouts make a 10 out of 10 combination.

prep time:
10 minutes

2 slices whole-grain bread

¼ cup hummus

⅓ cup greens of choice: arugula, spinach, or romaine

⅓ cup sliced cucumber

Half an avocado, thinly sliced

⅓ cup shredded carrots

3 sun-dried tomatoes, chopped

¼ cup alfalfa sprouts

Dijon mustard

1. Lightly toast the bread. Spread the hummus on the bottom piece of toast, and layer all of the veggies on top, starting with the greens and working your way up to the sprouts.

2. Spread the Dijon mustard on the other piece of toast, and put it on top.

3. Cut the sandwich in half and enjoy, Cali girl.

sf nf 20

sweet potato quesadilla

SERVES 1

If you need a quick, 10-minute meal that's actually filling, this quesadilla is going to be your new best friend. Instead of a traditional cheese quesadilla, this is made with vitamin A-rich sweet potato and fiber-filled refried beans. The longest-living people in the world eat beans daily, so make more plant-powered quesadillas for a health boost.

prep time:
5 minutes

cook time:
10 minutes

1 medium sweet potato

¼ tsp chili powder

2 tbsp nutritional yeast

Sprinkle of garlic powder

Pinch of salt and pepper

½ cup canned vegetarian refried beans

2 tbsp taco sauce

2 whole wheat tortillas

Olive oil spray

Optional toppings:

Pico de gallo

Sliced avocado

Dairy-free sour cream

1. Pierce the sweet potato with a fork a few times, then microwave it for 5 minutes or until tender.

2. Cut the sweet potato in half, and scoop out the insides of each half into a bowl, and mash. Add the chili powder, nutritional yeast, garlic powder, salt, and pepper.

3. Add the refried beans to a bowl and mix with the taco sauce.

4. Spread the bean mixture on half of each tortilla, and the sweet potato mixture on the other halves, then stick together.

5. Heat a pan to medium, spray with oil, then panfry the quesadilla for about 2 minutes on each side or until golden brown.

6. Cut the quesadilla into 4 or 6 pieces. Enjoy with the toppings of your choice!

greek salad pita

SERVES 3-4

Whenever I make this, I can't stop eating it. There's something about the warm pita, fresh veggies, creamy yogurt tzatziki, and herbed tofu feta that work so well together. Don't get too overwhelmed by the list of the ingredients; these only take about 20 minutes to make.

prep time:
20 minutes

1 cup diced cucumber

1 cup diced tomato

¼ cup diced red onion

¼ cup kalamata olives

¼ cup sliced pepperoncini or banana peppers

Pitas or wraps of your choice

Tofu feta:

½ block high-protein tofu, cubed

½ tbsp dried oregano

½ tbsp dried basil

2 tbsp olive oil

1 tbsp lemon juice

Pinch of salt, pepper, and garlic powder

Vegan 60-second tzatziki sauce:

1 cup plain vegan yogurt

½ cup chopped fresh dill

1 tbsp lemon juice

¼ tsp salt

¼ tsp garlic powder

Pinch of pepper

1. Add all the tofu feta ingredients into a large bowl. Let it marinate while you make the rest of this meal.

2. To a separate large bowl, add all of the veggies and mix together.

3. In a small bowl, mix the tzatziki sauce ingredients together.

4. Add the tofu feta to the veggies and mix.

5. Stuff the veggie and tofu feta mixture into a warmed pita and top with the vegan tzatziki.

roasted veggie wrap

SERVES 1

Can I just say, I *love* wraps. I have to confess, I actually like them better than sandwiches. The easiest way to make these wraps is to roast a ton of veggies in advance for the week so when you want to eat lunch, building the wrap only takes a few minutes. Trust me, having the veggies prepared beforehand is a game changer. Let's be honest, no one has time to wait for veggies to be done roasting during a work or school day.

prep time:
10 minutes

cook time:
20 minutes

½ zucchini, sliced

½ bell pepper, sliced

1 portobello mushroom, sliced

Olive oil

Sprinkle of salt and pepper

1 tbsp **Plant-Based Pesto Please** (page 76), or store-bought vegan pesto

1 large tortilla

¼ cup shredded purple cabbage

1 cup baby kale, or greens of choice

1. Preheat the oven to 425°F (220°C), and line a baking sheet with parchment paper. Feel free to use your air fryer for this if you have one!

2. Spread the sliced veggies out on the prepared baking sheet.

3. Drizzle olive oil over the veggies and sprinkle on the salt and pepper.

4. Roast for 20 minutes.

5. Spread the pesto onto the tortilla, add on the roasted veggies, shredded cabbage, and baby kale. Roll up tightly and enjoy!

HealthyGirl Tip

Add on some of your favorite grilled tofu for an extra protein boost!

eggless egg salad

SERVES 3

Never in a million years did I think it would be possible to make egg salad without any eggs, but it is, and the secret ingredient is tofu! I have been told by many egg-salad lovers that this plant-based version genuinely impressed them. They were even more impressed when I told them it's super high in protein too! If you make this in advance and keep it in the fridge, it's so easy to add it to a wrap or sandwich. Can you tell I am a huge fan of 5-minute lunches?

prep time:
10 minutes

1 block firm tofu

¼ cup vegan mayo

1 tsp Dijon mustard

1 tbsp yellow mustard

2 tbsp lemon juice

1 tsp turmeric

½ tsp garlic powder

½ tsp paprika

1 tsp salt

Pinch of pepper

¼ cup diced yellow onion

⅓ cup diced celery

¼ cup chopped fresh chives

¼ cup chopped fresh dill

1. Grab a large mixing bowl. Cut the tofu block in half. Cut one half into small cubes to act as the egg whites and set aside. Add the other uncut half into the mixing bowl.

2. Into the bowl, add the mayo, mustards, lemon juice, turmeric, garlic powder, paprika, salt, and pepper. Mash and mix together until creamy.

3. Add the onion, celery, chives, and dill, and the rest of the tofu cubes (egg whites) into the bowl and mix until combined.

4. Serve on a salad, with crackers, or on a sandwich!

bagel + carrot lox

SERVES 5

It's safe to say that if I had to plan my menu for my last day on Earth, a
bagel with lox would be on it. Eating lox for brunch is basically a Jewish girl's
rite of passage. I desperately wanted to make a plant-based version, and
this carrot lox does the trick. This bagel sandwich hits the damn spot.

prep time:
10 minutes

marinate:
overnight

Carrot lox:

3 large carrots

¼ cup caper or
pickle brine

2 tbsp capers

1 tbsp white miso
paste

1 sheet of nori
seaweed or
one 4-inch
piece
of kombu

3 tbsp olive oil

1 tsp chopped
fresh dill

2 tbsp lemon juice

1 tsp garlic
powder

½ tbsp soy sauce

1 tsp smoked
paprika

1 bagel

1–2 tbsp dairy-
free cream
cheese or
butter

2 large tomato
slices

6 thin cucumber
slices

3 slices red onion

1. Prep the carrot lox the day before.
   Bring a small pot of water to a boil.
   Use a peeler to make carrot ribbons.

2. Add the carrots to the boiling water
   for 2 minutes, then drain and rinse
   with cold water.

3. In a large container, add the rest of
   the carrot lox ingredients and mix.
   Add the carrots and mix again,
   making sure the carrots are
   completely covered.

4. Let the carrots marinate overnight.
   When you are ready to eat, remove
   the carrot lox from the brine.

5. Assemble your bagel with the other
   ingredients and eat up, bestie.

HealthyGirl Tip

If you have a mandoline, use it to slice
the carrots rather than a peeler—this
will make the slices the perfect
thickness.

no-fish tuna sandwich

SERVES 3–4

Raise your hand if you love tuna! This was one of the first plant-based recipes I learned how to make because I was tuna-obsessed and I needed to find a way to make a vegan version. You will see that I use chickpeas in a lot of my recipes, but it's because they're so versatile. They make the perfect high-protein, high-fiber tuna swap. Don't want to make this into a sandwich? It's also great on a salad or with crackers.

prep time: 10 minutes

1 (15 oz) can chickpeas, rinsed and drained

½ cup chopped dill pickles

¼ cup chopped red onion

2 tbsp tahini, plain vegan yogurt, or vegan mayo

⅓ cup shelled sunflower seeds

1 cup roughly chopped celery

1 tbsp dried dill

1 tsp Dijon mustard

2 slices of your favorite bread

Dill pickles

Lettuce

1. Add the chickpeas, pickles, onion, tahini, sunflower seeds, celery, dill, and mustard into a food processor and pulse until well combined. It should still have some texture to it and not be completely smooth.

2. Add onto your favorite bread with dill pickles and your favorite lettuce, and enjoy!

healthygirl snacks
munchies to graze on

gf   nb   sf   lf   20

busy girl energy bites

MAKES 15

I have been making these no-sugar-added energy bites for years. They have dried fruit, nut butter, nuts, and seeds, which help balance your blood sugar. The healthy fats in these will make sure this snack gives you a long-lasting boost of energy. This is a very functional snack, meaning it's packed with nutrients and it holds you over until your next meal. Just a few bites is the right amount to snack on between meals when you need a munchy.

prep time:
15 minutes

1 cup Medjool dates

½ cup raw cashews

½ cup raw almonds

½ cup dried unsweetened apricots

¼ cup raw pumpkin seeds

½ cup creamy natural peanut butter

Drop of pure vanilla extract

Pinch of salt

Shredded coconut

1. Add all the ingredients except for the coconut into a food processor.

2. Process ingredients until well combined.

3. Start forming the balls (you can make them as big or as small as you like), then roll them in the shredded coconut or dust with cacao powder.

HealthyGirl Tip

Substitute the apricots with raisins if you want the bites to be a bit sweeter.

foolproof air-popped popcorn

SERVES 1

I am addicted to popcorn. I am totally the girl who makes herself a huge bowl of popcorn and shoves popcorn in my mouth way too fast. Popcorn is a great low-calorie, high-fiber snack. Did you know you can make it in the microwave in a brown paper bag in under three minutes?

prep time:
5 minutes

3 tbsp organic popcorn kernels

Olive oil spray

Sea salt

1. Add the popcorn kernels to a brown paper lunch bag. Fold the bag closed at the top, and lay it flat in the microwave.

2. Microwave on high for 1 to 3 minutes. Stop the microwave when there's more than 2 seconds between pops.

3. Pour the popcorn into a bowl, spray on olive oil, and sprinkle on sea salt to taste.

> **HealthyGirl Tip**
> The size of the bag used will affect how long the popping takes. The larger the bag, the longer it will take to pop all the corn kernels.

diy trail mix

SERVES 4

Whenever you need a quick snack, you can make your own trail mix.
I recommend getting jars or containers, labeling them, and filling them with
your favorite dried fruit, nuts, seeds, and dark chocolate. Store-bought trail
mix often has a lot of added sugar and other additives, while DIY trail mix
allows you to control what ingredients you use. You can even make a bunch
of little bags or small containers of your own trail mix in advance for easy
grab-and-go snacking.

prep time:
5 minutes

Almonds

Cashews

Hazelnuts

Pumpkin seeds

Goji berries

Dark chocolate chips

1. Mix any combination of nuts, seeds, dried fruit, and chocolate together that you like.

2. Nibble on a handful or two for a great power-snack.

snack box

SERVES 1

A snack box is the kind of snack that keeps on giving because you can graze on it throughout the day. If you're someone who works outside the house or goes to school, you should make yourself a snack box to take with you. When you pack a snack box, pack a variety of fruits, veggies, nuts, and a high-protein option like edamame. Of course, it's a great idea to include a crunchy ingredient like pretzels or crackers too.

prep time:
5 minutes

Frozen edamame

Hot Girl Hummus
  (page 131)

Pretzels

Grapes

Almonds

Baby carrots

1. Prepare your box by first steaming frozen edamame in the microwave for 3 minutes or until cooked. Add them into the box.

2. Scoop Hot Girl Hummus into a small container. Add the pretzels next to the hummus.

3. Fill the rest of the box with grapes, almonds, and baby carrots.

4. Feel free to make a bunch for the week to have easy snacking at home or on the go.

rice cakes, 4 ways

SERVES 1

Rice cakes are underrated for snack time. I love that you can add any toppings you like, both sweet and savory. If you're in a pinch and need a healthy snack made in less than two minutes, this is going to be your new go-to. If you keep rice cakes and your favorite toppings on hand, you won't ever have to wonder what to make for a midday snack again.

prep time:
5 minutes

Strawberry Dream:
Strawberries + almond butter + ground cinnamon + poppy seeds

Hummus Girl:
Hot Girl Hummus (page 131) + tomato + sesame seeds

Avocado Bagel:
Avocado + cucumber + dill + everything bagel seasoning

PB Love:
Peanut butter + banana + cacao nibs

1. Top your rice cakes with your desired toppings and enjoy.

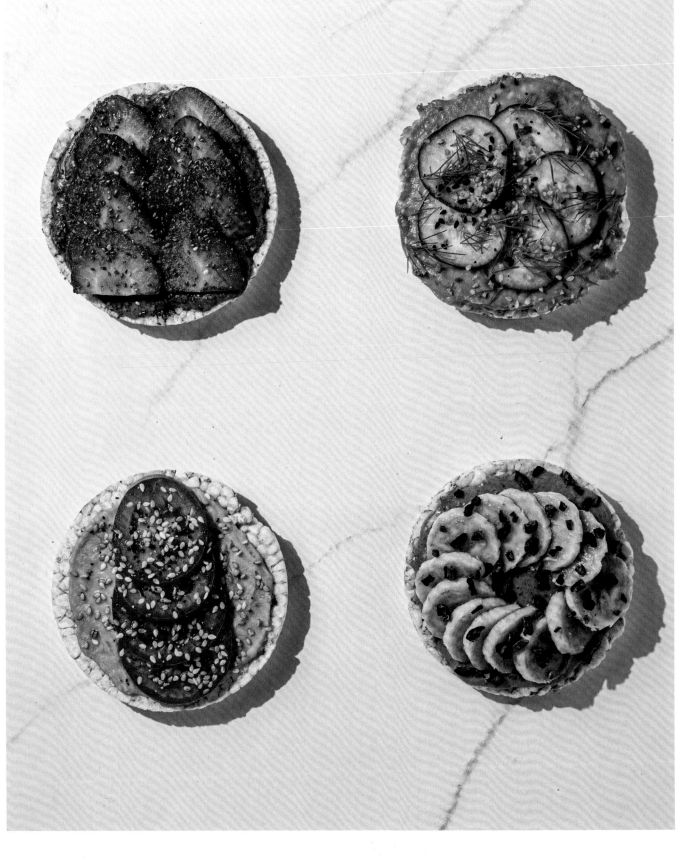

hot girl hummus

SERVES 8

Homemade hummus is actually way easier to make than you'd think. All you do is add all of the ingredients into a food processor and blend until smooth. Adding ice cubes is an ancient middle eastern secret to making the hummus extra creamy and smooth. Trust me on this one. Add this hummus to bowls, eat with veggies or crackers, or pair with some warm pita. You can also make a grazing board to eat with it, which is so fun and yummy!

prep time:
10 minutes

1 (15 oz) can of chickpeas, rinsed and drained

¼ cup olive oil

⅓ cup tahini

⅓ cup lemon juice

2 cloves garlic

1 tsp salt

5–8 ice cubes

smoked paprika, for topping

extra chickpeas, for topping

1. Blend the chickpeas, olive oil, tahini, lemon juice, garlic, and salt together in a food processor until smooth.

2. Scrape down the sides and add the ice cubes. Blend for 1 to 2 minutes until totally smooth.

3. Top with smoked paprika and any extra chickpeas as you like!

high-protein edamame hummus

SERVES 8

Edamame is an amazing source of plant protein that has even more protein than chickpeas. This high-protein version of hummus makes for a filling, yummy snack. Make a batch of edamame hummus for easy, convenient snacking throughout the week.

prep time:
5 minutes

cook time:
5 minutes

12 oz package frozen shelled edamame

⅓ cup tahini

3 cloves garlic

3 tbsp lemon juice

2 tbsp olive oil

1 tsp salt

5–8 ice cubes

1. Microwave the shelled edamame in a bowl (according to the bag's instructions).

2. Blend the edamame, tahini, garlic, lemon juice, olive oil, and salt together in a food processor until smooth.

3. Scrape down the sides, and add the ice cubes. Blend for 1 to 2 minutes until totally smooth.

4. Serve with veggies, crackers, or bread—you name it.

(gf) (sf) (nf) (lf)

homemade pickles

SERVES 8

Pickles are so crave worthy. They're just the perfect crunchy, salty, and savory little snack. I bought $10 pickles at the grocery store, and then made my own to compare. This recipe is without a doubt better than the expensive pickles from the market.

prep time:
5 minutes

cook time:
5 minutes

5 Persian cucumbers

Handful of fresh dill

1 tsp mustard seeds

1 tsp peppercorns

3 cloves garlic

1 cup water

1 tsp salt

1 cup distilled white vinegar

1 tbsp cane sugar

1. Slice off ⅛-inch from the blossom end of the cucumber to prevent mushy pickles.

2. Cut the cucumbers lengthwise into quarters, and add them to a tall jar or glass container. Add the dill, mustard seeds, peppercorns, and garlic cloves.

3. In a small pot, bring the water, salt, vinegar, and sugar to near boiling. The mixture should get hot enough to dissolve the salt and sugar, but not to a boiling point.

4. Pour the liquid over the cucumbers into the jar. Seal the jar tightly with a lid and refrigerate. The pickles will be ready to eat the next day!

5. Store in the refrigerator for up to a few weeks.

yogurt parfait to-go

SERVES 1

A yogurt parfait is a great gut-friendly snack for a quick boost of energy, protein, healthy fats, and carbs. The berries and chia seeds contain high levels of fiber, which prevents constipation. Yogurt is fermented, which means it contains probiotics that are amazing for keeping your gut microbiome healthy and thriving.

prep time:
5 minutes

1 cup vegan yogurt

¼ cup granola

1 cup berries of choice

1 tsp chia seeds

1. Layer a jar or container with the vegan yogurt, granola, berries, and chia seeds.

healthygirl comfort food

for getting through your toughest days

nourish your soul veggie bowl

SERVES 2

There is a common misconception that comfort food can't be healthy. Once I teach you how to make more meals like this warming, healing veggie bowl, I will change your mind. There is something so nourishing and comforting about roasted veggies, deliciously baked sweet potato, hearty quinoa, and creamy tahini dressing.

prep time:
10 minutes

cook time:
30 minutes

1 large sweet potato, cubed

½ head cauliflower, cut into florets

2 cups cherry tomatoes

Olive oil spray

½ tsp salt

¼ tsp pepper

½ tsp garlic powder

1 cup quinoa

2 cups finely chopped kale

1 batch **Maple Dijon Tahini Dressing** (page 77)

1. Preheat the oven to 400°F (200°C), and line a baking sheet with parchment paper.

2. Place the sweet potato, cauliflower, and tomatoes on the prepared baking sheet.

3. Spray the veggies with olive oil spray, and sprinkle on the salt, pepper, and garlic powder.

4. Bake for 30 minutes or until the veggies are cooked.

5. While that bakes, cook the quinoa according to the package instructions.

6. Sauté the kale in a pan for a few minutes in a little olive oil, then season with a little salt and pepper.

7. Assemble each bowl with quinoa on the bottom, then add the roasted veggies, kale, and as much dressing as you like. Save the rest of the dressing in the fridge.

spicy cozy ramen

SERVES 2–3

This easy, at-home ramen is beyond yummy. Ramen was created when this unique Chinese noodle dish fused with Japanese cuisine. It is said that ramen has unlimited variations, and that all you need is five main ingredients: noodles, soup stock, veggies, sauce, and fat or oil.

cook time:
25 minutes

4 cups veggie broth

1 piece kombu

1 tbsp white miso paste

1 cup water

1 tbsp toasted sesame oil

1 tbsp soy sauce

1 tsp minced or grated fresh ginger

1–2 cloves garlic, minced

1½ tsp sriracha

1 cup bok choy leaves

1 cup sliced shiitake mushrooms

½ cup frozen corn

1 (8 oz) package ramen noodles (frozen or dried)

Garnish:

Mung bean sprouts

Cilantro

Scallions

Red pepper flakes

1. Add the veggie broth into a soup pot and bring it to medium-high heat.

2. Rinse the kombu and add it into the pot.

3. Mix the miso paste into the water in a small bowl to dissolve it, then set aside.

4. To the soup pot, add the toasted sesame oil, soy sauce, ginger, garlic, and sriracha.

5. Add the bok choy, mushrooms, and corn.

6. Right before the mixture boils, remove the kombu.

7. Once boiling, turn down to a simmer for 20 minutes.

8. In a separate pot, cook the ramen noodles according to the package instructions. When they are finished, divide them up into 2 to 3 bowls.

9. Once the ramen is done simmering, ladle some of the broth into a small bowl, mix it with the miso, then add it all back into the pot and stir.

10. Ladle the soup over the noodles along with the cooked veggies, then top with mung bean sprouts, cilantro, scallions, and red pepper flakes.

warm + creamy mushroom risotto

SERVES 2

I know risotto seems time consuming and complicated, but it actually takes less than 50 minutes to make. You are going to feel so professional once you make this at home because it tastes way too good to be true. Here's the plan: make yourself a bowl of risotto at the end of a long day (because it's truly the ultimate comfort food), and binge-watch your current favorite series.

prep time:
15 minutes

cook time:
30 minutes

5 cups veggie broth, divided

1 yellow onion, finely diced

3 cloves garlic, minced

2 tbsp olive oil

1½ cups sliced cremini mushrooms

1½ cup sliced white button mushrooms

1 cup arborio rice

½ cup white wine

1 tsp salt, divided

2 tbsp nutritional yeast

¼ tsp pepper

Garnish:

2 tbsp chopped Italian flat-leaf parsley

Vegan parmesan (optional)

1. Heat the veggie broth in a soup pot on medium heat to keep it hot for the risotto.

2. In a large pan, sauté the onion and garlic in the olive oil on medium heat for a few minutes.

3. Add the sliced mushrooms into the pan, and sauté on medium-high heat until the water has cooked out of the mushrooms (about 10 minutes).

4. Add the rice into the pan, and sauté for one minute.

5. Deglaze the pan with white wine, and reduce the wine until it's evaporated.

6. Add 2 cups of the hot veggie broth and ¼ teaspoon of salt. Reduce to medium heat, and stir every minute or so until the liquid is mostly absorbed.

7. Add the remaining 3 cups of hot broth, 1 cup at a time, and another ¼ teaspoon of salt with each cup, allowing each round to absorb before adding more broth. Make sure to stir regularly.

8. The rice should be tender when it's done. You can taste it to make sure. Still al dente? Add more broth or water until it's cooked to your liking

9. Once the liquid is absorbed about 95 percent of the way, add the nutritional yeast and pepper, and stir.

10. Serve with fresh parsley on top and vegan parmesan (if using).

hearty lentil bolognese

SERVES 4

This is your sign to include lentils in more of your meals. Lentils are basically a plant-based protein powerhouse, packing 18 grams per cup. If you love pasta with meat sauce, this is going to be your new favorite dinner. Bolognese made with lentils, mushrooms, zucchini, and carrots makes for a surprisingly filling and crave-worthy dinner.

prep time:
15 minutes

cook time:
30 minutes

1 (16 oz) package of pasta

½ cup pasta water

1 cup finely diced yellow onion

3 cloves garlic, minced

1 tbsp olive oil

1 cup finely grated carrots

1 cup finely diced mushrooms

1 zucchini, finely diced

1 (32 oz) jar marinara sauce

4 cups cooked brown lentils

Salt and pepper, to taste

Garnish:

Freshly chopped basil or parsley

Vegan parmesan

1. Bring a large pot of water to a boil and salt it. Cook the pasta to your liking. When done, reserve some of the pasta water and set aside.

2. In a large pan, on medium heat, sauté the onion and garlic in the olive oil until translucent.

3. Add the carrots, mushrooms, and zucchini into the pan, and sauté for 10 minutes or until the moisture cooks out.

4. Pour in the marinara sauce and lentils. Cover and simmer for 10 to 15 minutes, stirring occasionally. Season the sauce with salt and pepper.

5. Add the reserved pasta water into the sauce. Use tongs or a slotted spoon to remove the pasta from the pot, and add into the pan with the sauce. Gently combine. Garnish and serve!

cheesy girl lasagna

SERVES 6

You won't believe this lasagna is dairy-free. The homemade tofu ricotta is super high in plant-based protein, but it also perfectly mimics ricotta cheese. I know so many people with a dairy intolerance who still want to enjoy a cheesy, rich lasagna. I got you. Everyone I make this for asks me for the recipe. Make this on Sunday and heat for dinners for the week ahead.

prep time:
15 minutes

cook time:
55 minutes

2 (32 oz) jars marinara sauce, divided

1–2 packages regular lasagna noodles, uncooked

Vegan parmesan

Tofu ricotta:

2 (16 oz) packages firm tofu

⅓ cup nutritional yeast

1 cup fresh basil leaves

1 tbsp dried oregano

4 tbsp lemon juice

2 cloves garlic, minced

1 tsp salt

1. Preheat the oven to 375°F (190°C).

2. Prepare the tofu ricotta by adding all the ingredients into a food processor. Blend until creamy and well combined.

3. Prep a 9 x 13-inch baking dish by adding about ½ cup of the marinara sauce and 2 tablespoons of water to the bottom of it. Spread it around evenly.

4. Add a layer of 4 lasagna noodles (or however many you can fit). Next, add a couple dollops of tofu ricotta, then add some marinara sauce, and spread it around generously.

5. Repeat this process, adding layers until you run out of ricotta cheese. Top the lasagna with a layer of marinara sauce and a generous sprinkle of vegan parmesan.

6. Cover with foil, and bake for 40 minutes, covered, then 15 minutes, uncovered. A fork should easily pierce through the layers when it's done.

hug-in-a-bowl penne alla vodka

SERVES 4

When I think of comfort food, I immediately think of a big-ass bowl of pasta. You won't believe how creamy coconut milk can make a pasta dish. Coconut milk also has healthy fats, which we love. Guess what? This only takes 20 minutes to make. Cozy up and enjoy. I promise it will make your day better

cook time:
20 minutes

1 (16 oz) box of penne

½ yellow onion, finely diced

4 cloves garlic, minced

2 tbsp olive oil

1 cup vodka

1 (24 oz) jar tomato sauce

¾ cup full-fat coconut milk

½ tsp salt

Pinch of pepper

Garnish:

Vegan parmesan

Fresh flat-leaf parsley

Red pepper flakes

1. Bring a large pot of water to a boil and salt it. Cook the penne according to package instructions.

2. While the pasta cooks, in a large saucepan, sauté the onion and garlic in the olive oil on medium heat for a few minutes.

3. Add the vodka and let it reduce and simmer for 3 to 4 minutes, stirring every 30 seconds.

4. Pour the tomato sauce into the pan. Open the can of coconut milk, and scrape the fat off the top and pour this full-fat into the pan. Stir until well combined.

5. Add salt and pepper, and simmer for 5 minutes.

6. When the pasta is done cooking, drain and add directly into the sauce.

7. Garnish with vegan parmesan, parsley, and red pepper flakes if you want a little kick.

life-changing baked mac + cheese

SERVES 6–8

Raise your hand if you're a mac and cheese girl! This creamy, heavenly, cheesy mac and cheese is made with sweet potatoes and cashews. Cashews are basically magical because, when blended, they can turn a sauce into plant-based creamy perfection. Whether you make a pan for your family, for a girls' night in, or just for yourself to have for the week, you're going to crave this all the time.

prep time:
5 minutes

cook time:
35 minutes

1 large sweet potato

1 cup raw cashews

1 (12 oz) box elbow macaroni noodles

¼ cup nutritional yeast

1 cup nondairy milk

½ cup cooking liquid from sweet potato

½ tsp Dijon mustard

1 tsp miso paste

¼ tsp pepper

½ tsp smoked paprika

½ tsp garlic powder

1 tsp salt

2 tbsp olive oil

½ cup bread crumbs

1. Preheat the oven to 400°F (200°C).

2. Bring two pots of water to a boil: one for the sweet potato and cashews and one for the macaroni.

3. While you wait, peel and cut the sweet potato into large cubes. Add them to one of the pots of water along with the cashews. Once boiling, cook for 10 minutes, or until the potato is fork-tender.

4. Salt the boiling water in the other pot, and cook the macaroni until al dente.

5. While these cook, add the following to a blender: nutritional yeast, nondairy milk, cooking liquid from the sweet potato, Dijon mustard, miso paste, pepper, smoked paprika, garlic powder, and salt. Blend until a completely smooth cheesy sauce is achieved.

6. Add the cashews and potato to the blender. Blend until completely smooth.

7. Drain the pasta and add to a 9 x 13-inch casserole dish. Pour the cheesy sauce on top and mix well.

8. In a small bowl, mix together the olive oil and bread crumbs. Top the mac and cheese with the bread crumbs and bake on the bottom rack for 7 minutes.

9. Move the mac and cheese to the top rack, and broil for 3 to 4 minutes or until golden brown. Be careful not to burn it.

sweet potato gnocchi

SERVES 2

This has to be one of the most perfect comforting fall dinners for date night. If I'm ever having a bad day, my husband will suggest we make sweet potato gnocchi together for dinner. Not only is it a fun, stress-relieving activity to do together that will brighten up any day, but the result is also restaurant worthy.

prep time:
20 minutes

cook time:
15 minutes

1 large sweet potato

1 cup flour (gluten-free or all-purpose flour)

¼ tsp salt

2 tbsp olive oil

3 cloves garlic, minced

1 tsp finely chopped fresh rosemary

2 leaves fresh sage, finely chopped

1 tsp fresh thyme leaves

¼ cup finely chopped pecans

Salt and pepper, to taste

Vegan parmesan (optional)

1. Microwave the sweet potato until tender (6 to 8 minutes).

2. Let it cool for a few minutes, then peel the skin off. Mash enough to make 1 cup.

3. Bring a large pot of water to a boil, and salt the water generously.

4. In a bowl, combine the flour, mashed sweet potato and salt. When the mixture is cool enough, use your hands to mix and form into a ball. The dough should not be sticky or crumbly. If it's too sticky, add more flour 1 tablespoon at a time. If it's too dry, add more cooked and mashed sweet potato.

5. On a lightly floured cutting board, cut each dough ball in half. Roll each half into a long log. Cut the log into about 16 even "gnocchi pillow" pieces.

6. Add the gnocchi to the pot of salted boiling water and cook for about 4 minutes. They will float to the top.

7. While the gnocchi cooks, heat a pan to medium. Add the olive oil, garlic, and herbs. Sauté for a few minutes, then add the pecans and cook for another minute. When the gnocchi is done, using a slotted spoon, transfer the gnocchi directly into the pan.

8. Sauté for a few more minutes, season with salt and pepper, then serve fresh with vegan parmesan (if using).

healthygirl dinners

never wonder what to make for dinner again

garlic alfredo pasta

SERVES 4

Did you know you can make creamy, indulgent alfredo sauce without any cheese or dairy? Cashews are the secret to making many plant-based creamy sauces, including this alfredo. A little miso helps to bring out the flavors in the sauce. I like to serve with fettuccine, but you can use any pasta you like.

prep time:
10 minutes

cook time:
20 minutes

1 (16 oz) package fettuccine

½ cup diced onion

1 tbsp minced garlic

1 tbsp olive oil

1½ cups raw cashews

2½ cups pasta water, divided

1 tsp white miso paste

3 tbsp lemon juice

2 tbsp nutritional yeast

1 tsp salt

¼ tsp pepper

Garnish:

Fresh parsley

Lemon zest

Vegan parmesan

1. Bring a large pot of water to a boil and salt generously. Cook the pasta according to the package instructions. When it's done, drain and reserve 2½ cups of the pasta water.

2. In a large pan, sauté the onion and garlic in olive oil on medium heat until translucent.

3. To a blender, add the onion, garlic, cashews, 2 cups of pasta water, miso paste, lemon juice, nutritional yeast, salt, and pepper. Blend until smooth.

4. Add the pasta back into the pot, pour the sauce over it, add the remaining ½ cup of pasta water, and toss gently with tongs while on medium heat.

5. Serve in pasta bowls and garnish with parsley, lemon zest, and vegan parmesan (homemade or store-bought).

lemon caper tofu filets

SERVES 2

Looks like fish, right? It's crazy what you can do with tofu. This is a plant-based main course that is a serious showstopper. My husband used to be the biggest meat-eater, but now he loves tofu (especially this recipe).

prep time:
5 minutes

cook time:
15 minutes

1 block extra-firm tofu

Salt and pepper, to taste

2 tbsp olive oil, divided

1 cup finely diced yellow onion

4 cloves garlic, minced

½ cup white wine

2 tbsp lemon juice

1 tbsp lemon zest

2 tbsp capers

2 tbsp chopped flat-leaf parsley

Garnish:

Lemon slices

Fresh dill

1. Cut the block of tofu into 6 slices, make diagonal slits down each piece, and season with salt and pepper on each side.

2. Heat a large pan on medium heat, and add 1 tablespoon of the olive oil into the pan.

3. Pat the tofu slices dry, then add them into the pan and cook for 5 minutes on each side until golden brown. Remove the tofu from the pan and set aside. In the same pan, add the onion, garlic, and the remaning 1 tablespoon of oil, and sauté until translucent.

4. Add the wine, lemon juice, and lemon zest, and let it simmer for a few minutes.

5. Add the capers, parsley, and salt and pepper, to taste.

6. Put the tofu back into the pan, and simmer for a few minutes until the tofu is warmed in the sauce.

HealthyGirl Tip

I suggest serving with asparagus to make the perfect dinner combination.

peanut veggie stir-fry

SERVES 3

I am promising you now that this peanut stir-fry is going to become a part of your weekly dinner rotation. It's easy to make and has ingredients you probably already have on hand, and everyone loves it. This is the kind of dinner that you make when you have twenty minutes to throw something together. Feel free to add tofu or tempeh to this for a protein boost

prep time:
10 minutes

cook time:
10 minutes

1 tbsp sesame or olive oil

1 cup diced yellow onion

3 cloves garlic, minced

1 red bell pepper, sliced

2 cups sliced shiitake mushrooms

2 cups broccoli florets

1 cup halved sugar snap peas

1 cup white or brown rice, cooked according to package instructions

Heavenly peanut sauce:

¼ cup peanut butter

2 tbsp water

2 tbsp soy sauce

1 tbsp toasted sesame oil

2 tbsp rice vinegar

1 tsp sriracha

1 tsp ground ginger

1 tsp garlic powder

1. Heat a large pan or wok to medium heat.

2. Add the oil, onion, and garlic, and sauté for a few minutes until slightly browned.

3. Transfer all of the veggies into the pan, and sauté for about 5 to 7 minutes until tender. Don't overcook.

4. Make the peanut sauce by whisking all the ingredients together in a bowl or cup.

5. Pour the sauce over the veggies while they are in the pan, and stir until warmed thoroughly and combined. Serve over rice and enjoy!

better-than-takeout sesame tofu

SERVES 2

When I made this for my friend she said, "This is literally better than takeout," and immediately asked for the recipe. This sesame tofu is crispy, flavorful, and drool-worthy. One of the number one comments I hear about tofu is that people don't know how to cook it and that it never turns out right. This is the recipe for you if you want to fall in love with tofu.

prep time:
10 minutes

cook time:
10 minutes

1 block high-protein tofu, cubed

2 tablespoons cornstarch

1 tbsp sesame oil

1 head steamed broccoli

1 cup brown rice, cooked according to package instructions

Garnish:
Scallions
Sesame seeds

Secret sauce:

¼ cup coconut aminos

1 tbsp soy sauce

1 tbsp toasted sesame oil

1 tsp rice vinegar

1 tbsp maple syrup

½ tsp chili garlic sauce

1 tsp garlic powder

½ tsp ground ginger

1. In a medium bowl, mix the tofu cubes with cornstarch.

2. Heat a pan to medium heat. Once heated, add the sesame oil and tofu. Panfry, flipping and stirring as necessary until all sides are golden brown.

3. Whisk all the sauce ingredients in a bowl.

4. Once the tofu is brown, turn the heat to low and pour the secret sauce into the pan. Stir and combine with the tofu until the sauce thickens, about 5 minutes.

5. Serve the tofu with the broccoli and brown rice. Sprinkle on scallions and sesame seeds.

gf · sf · nf · lf

easy chickpea coconut curry

SERVES 2–3

One of my favorite things to do is make this curry for dinner and have my husband, Ari, pick up roti (whole wheat flatbread) from our local Indian restaurant. I am all about fast dinners and while homemade bread would be nice, picking some up for a few dollars is the best hack. The hearty chickpeas, creamy coconut milk, and flavorful spices make this dish so incredibly warming and delicious. It's a party in your mouth!

prep time:
10 minutes

cook time:
20 minutes

1 yellow onion, diced

2 cloves garlic, minced

1 tbsp olive oil

1 tbsp curry powder

1 tsp ground cumin

1 (15 oz) can crushed tomatoes

1 (14 oz) can full-fat coconut milk

2 (15 oz) cans chickpeas, rinsed and drained

½ tsp salt, plus more to taste

¼ tsp pepper

¼ tsp red pepper flakes

1 cup uncooked basmati rice

Juice of 1 lime

Cilantro for garnish

1. In a deep pan, sauté the onion and garlic in olive oil on medium heat until lightly browned. Add the curry and cumin, and sauté for a minute.

2. Pour in the tomatoes, coconut milk, chickpeas, salt, and pepper. Stir.

3. Simmer for 10 minutes, uncovered, stirring halfway through. Sprinkle in red pepper flakes at the end.

4. Cook the basmati rice according to package instructions as the curry simmers.

5. Serve the curry with rice. Drizzle the lime juice on the curry to bring out the flavors, and garnish with cilantro.

HealthyGirl Tip
Feel free to add more red pepper flakes if you like it spicy!

---

meal prep fajita bowls

SERVES 4

These fajita bowls are the best dinner to meal prep in advance because they're still great reheated days later. There are certain foods that are not meant to be kept as leftovers, but this one is a winner. These come in super handy when you need easy, ready-to-go meals that can be popped in the microwave at a moment's notice.

prep time:
10 minutes

cook time:
15 minutes

1 tbsp lime juice

½ cup finely chopped cilantro

1 cup rice, cooked according to package instructions

1 white onion, sliced

1 red bell pepper, sliced

1 yellow bell pepper, sliced

1 tbsp olive oil

2 tsp chili powder

1 tsp smoked paprika

1 tsp garlic powder

1 tsp ground cumin

1 tsp coriander

Salt and pepper, to taste

1 (15 oz) can black beans, rinsed and drained

1. Add the lime juice and cilantro to the cooked rice.

2. In a large pan, sauté the onion and peppers in olive oil on medium heat. Sauté for about 5 minutes then add chili powder, smoked paprika, garlic powder, cumin, coriander and salt and pepper, to taste.

3. Sauté for another 5 minutes or until the peppers and onions are tender and cooked through. Add a splash of water to the pan if the onions and peppers start sticking to the pan.

4. You will need four containers. Evenly divide up the peppers, rice, and beans into each container, and enjoy for dinners throughout the week.

HealthyGirl Tip
Some optional fresh toppings for this recipe could be grape tomatoes, avocado, and your favorite salsa.

black bean babe tacos

SERVES 5

Growing up, when my mom would decide it was "taco night," she would always make ground beef with taco seasoning. My vegan tacos aren't made with meat, but with black beans and quinoa—a heart-healthy, fiber-rich alternative. The best part is that the taco filling is made in one pot, and while it cooks you can prep the fresh ingredients.

prep time:
10 minutes

cook time:
15 minutes

½ yellow onion, diced

1 tbsp olive oil or avocado oil

2 tsp chili powder

1 tsp smoked paprika

1 tsp garlic powder

1 tsp ground cumin

1 cup quinoa

1½ cups water

1 can mild green chilies

1 (15 oz) can black beans, rinsed and drained

1 (8 oz) can tomato sauce

½ tsp salt, plus more to taste

8 corn tortillas

1–2 avocados, sliced

1 cup shredded purple cabbage

½ cup chopped cilantro

Vegan sour cream

Lime

1. In a saucepan, add the onion, oil, and spices, and sauté on medium heat for a few minutes.

2. Add the quinoa, water, green chilies, black beans, tomato sauce, and salt. Stir and bring to a boil. Cover and simmer for 15 minutes or until the liquid is absorbed and the quinoa is fluffy.

3. While this cooks, warm the corn tortillas in a pan or in the microwave. Fill the tortillas with the quinoa taco filling, avocado, purple cabbage, and cilantro.

4. Top with vegan sour cream and freshly squeezed lime juice.

> **HealthyGirl Tip**
> You can always cut up more or less of the fresh ingredients depending on how many tacos you're making. Cooking for one or two? Store the rest of the taco filling in the fridge if there are leftovers.

rainbow peanut noodles

SERVES 4

These vegan rainbow peanut noodles make the easiest 25-minute dinner. If you're trying to eat healthier but don't know where to start, this simple plant-based noodle dish is easy to make and tastes out-of-this-world amazing. This is one of those meals that makes delicious cold leftovers too!

prep time:
15 minutes

cook time:
10 minutes

1 (12 oz) box thin whole wheat spaghetti noodles

1 cup frozen shelled edamame

1½ cups sliced red bell pepper

1 cup shredded purple cabbage

1 cup carrot ribbons

½ cup chopped cilantro

1 cup fresh spinach

1 batch **Sesame Peanut Dressing** (page 78)

Sesame seeds for garnish

1. Bring a large pot of water to a boil and salt it. Cook the spaghetti noodles according to package instructions. When they are done, drain and rinse with cold water.

2. While the noodles are cooking, microwave the frozen edamame for 3 minutes or until cooked.

3. To a large serving bowl, add the noodles, edamame, bell pepper, cabbage, carrots, cilantro, spinach, and Sesame Peanut Dressing.

4. Use tongs to toss, and sprinkle on sesame seeds.

HealthyGirl Tip
Instead of microwaving the edamame, you can also pour boiling water over them and let them sit while you prep the other veggies, then drain them.

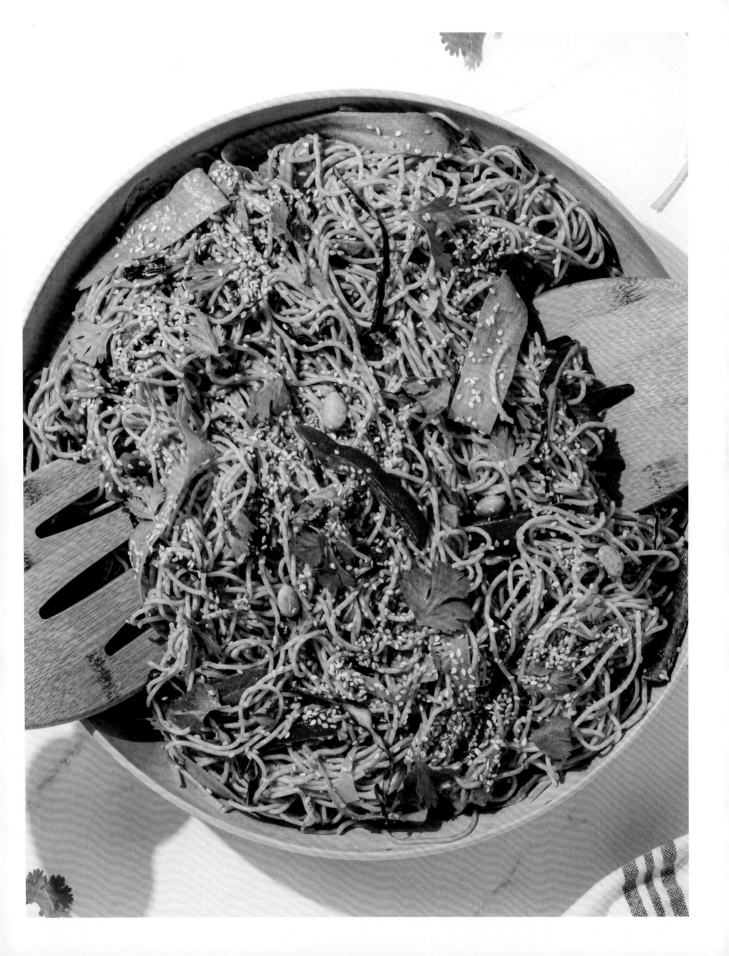

crispy no-chicken tenders (with baked fries)

SERVES 3–4

Chicken tenders and fries are such a classic combination. You'd never guess that tofu can be turned into the crispiest, most satisfying plant-based chicken tenders. I highly recommend making these in the air fryer. The honeyless mustard complements them perfectly.

prep time:
20 minutes

cook time:
35 minutes

1 block high-protein tofu (the firmest tofu)

½ cup chickpea flour

⅔ cup water

½ cup bread crumbs

⅓ cup sesame seeds

1 tsp paprika

1 tsp garlic powder

½ tsp onion powder

½ tsp salt

¼ tsp pepper

Olive oil spray

Baked fries:

3 russet potatoes

2 tbsp olive oil

1 tsp salt

¼ tsp pepper

1 tsp garlic powder

Honeyless mustard:

⅓ cup Dijon or yellow mustard

2 tbsp maple syrup

Chicken Instructions:

1. Preheat an air fryer or oven to 400°F (200°C). Break the tofu into nugget- or tender-like shapes (not too big), about the length of your thumb.

2. Prepare one bowl with the chickpea flour and water. Mix together.

3. Prepare another bowl with the bread crumbs, sesame seeds, and spices. Mix together.

4. Pat the tofu dry. Dip each piece of tofu in the chickpea flour mixture, then roll in the bread crumb mixture until coated. Place in the air fryer.

5. Spray the nuggets with olive oil spray. Bake in the air fryer for 8 to 10 minutes or until golden brown. Nuggets should be turned once, for even crispiness.

6. If using an oven, bake on parchment paper at 400°F (200°C) for 30 minutes, flipping over halfway through, or until golden brown.

7. Whisk the mustard and maple syrup together in a small bowl to make the honeyless mustard.

Fries Instructions:

1. Preheat the oven to 400°F (200°C), and line a baking sheet with parchment paper.

2. Cut the potatoes into fries, then add onto the preparedbaking sheet. Drizzle on the olive oil and seasonings. Mix well.

3. Bake for 35 minutes or until golden brown.

olive, shroom + artichoke pizza

SERVES 4

This is my go-to dinner when we've had a super-busy day and we want something quick and easy for the two of us to eat. I love pairing this pizza with a big, chopped salad too! Make this pizza for a cute weeknight date, for your bestie, to share with your roommate, or just to enjoy by yourself. Sometimes we all need a self-care night with pizza, a face mask, and a glass of wine.

prep time:
15 minutes

cook time:
10 minutes

1 store-bought pizza crust

1 batch **Plant-Based Pesto Please** (page 76)

1 cup sliced baby bella mushrooms

½ cup sliced kalamata olives

½ cup sliced green olives

1 cup marinated artichoke hearts, drained

Garnish:

Fresh basil

Red pepper flakes

Vegan parmesan

1. Preheat the oven to 450°F (230°C).

2. Place the pizza crust on a baking sheet lined with parchment paper, or a round nonstick pizza pan sprayed with olive oil.

3. Add as much Plant-Based Pesto Please as you want to the crust. Add more if you like it saucier.

4. Top the pizza with the mushrooms, olives, and artichoke hearts.

5. Bake the crust until it's to your desired crispness. Garnish with fresh basil, red pepper flakes, and vegan parmesan, then cut the pizza and dig in.

healthygirl side dishes

great for gatherings or to pair with dinner

(gf) (sf) (20)

quick strawberry arugula side salad

SERVES 4

Sometimes the best side dish at dinner is a gorgeous, fresh salad. The sweet strawberries work perfectly with the spicy, slightly bitter arugula, crisp cucumbers, crunchy almonds, and creamy feta. I love a simple salad like this that tastes like it took you hours to make, but really only took fifteen minutes.

prep time:
15 minutes

3 cups fresh spinach

3 cups arugula

1½ cups sliced strawberries

1 cup sliced cucumbers

½ cup sliced red onion

⅓ cup slivered almonds

½ cup vegan feta

1 batch **Basic Balsamic Vinaigrette** (page 75)

1. Add the spinach, arugula, strawberries, cucumbers, and red onion into a large salad serving bowl.

2. Sprinkle on slivered almonds and vegan feta.

3. Add as much or as little of the dressing as you want. I suggest keeping it on the side so that you can save any leftovers.

roasted rainbow veggies

SERVES 3–4

You should definitely know how to make a pan of roasted veggies, and I am going to teach you how. Have you ever heard that you should eat the rainbow? When making veggies, I recommend using a variety of veggies of different colors. The color actually says a lot about the kind of nutrients you receive from eating it. For example, dark red veggies like beets are packed with folate, and yellow and orange veggies are high in vitamin A.

prep time:
10 minutes

cook time:
30 minutes

1 cup mixed color cherry tomatoes

1 yellow bell pepper, sliced

1 yellow squash, cut in half circles

1 zucchini, cut in half circles

1 cup halved Brussels sprouts

1 carrot, sliced

½ red onion, sliced

1 cup sliced beets

2 tbsp olive oil

1 tsp salt

¼ tsp pepper

½ tsp garlic powder

½ tsp dried thyme

1. Preheat the oven to 425°F (220°C), and line a baking sheet with parchment paper, or use a casserole dish.

2. Add the veggies to the prepared baking sheet. Toss them with the olive oil and seasonings until evenly coated. Roast for 30 minutes and serve.

HealthyGirl Tip
Arrange the veggies by color to serve them in a fun rainbow pattern!

maple balsamic winter veggies

SERVES 4

This is a great veggie medley to make in the fall and winter because the butternut squash and Brussels sprouts will be in their seasonal prime. Balsamic vinegar and maple syrup are a great combination of sweet and savory flavors that will make you actually want to eat your veggies.

prep time:
10 minutes

cook time:
35 minutes

3 cups halved Brussels sprouts

1 red onion, chopped

1 (20 oz) bag frozen cubed butternut squash or 3 cups fresh

3 tbsp balsamic vinegar

3 tbsp maple syrup

2 tbsp olive oil

1 tsp garlic powder

1 tsp salt

¼ tsp pepper

2 tbsp balsamic glaze

1. Preheat the oven to 400°F (200°C). Line a baking sheet with parchment paper.

2. Add the Brussels sprouts, red onion, and squash to the prepared pan, and pour the balsamic vinegar, maple syrup, olive oil, and spices on top. Mix well so they are evenly coated.

3. Bake for 30 minutes, stirring halfway through, until golden and tender.

4. Add the balsamic glaze to the veggies when they come out of the oven for extra, sticky sweetness, and mix. Pop them back in the oven for 5 minutes to caramelize the glaze.

perfectly roasted spaghetti squash

SERVES 6

Can we just give a shout out to Mother Nature for creating a squash that mimics spaghetti? It's delicious, fun to eat, and high in fiber, vitamin B6, vitamin A, and vitamin C. This makes a warm, beautiful side dish, or you can even eat it as a pasta substitute with pesto or Bolognese sauce!

prep time:
5 minutes

cook time:
40 minutes

1 spaghetti squash

2 tbsp olive oil

1 tsp salt

¼ tsp pepper

1. Preheat the oven to 425°F (220°C). Line a baking sheet with parchment paper.

2. Cut the spaghetti squash in half lengthwise, and scrape the seeds out using a spoon.

3. Place each half of the squash, cut side up, on the prepared baking sheet. Drizzle the olive oil evenly over both halves. Season both halves evenly with the salt and pepper. Turn the squash halves over to roast with the cut side facing down.

4. Bake for 30 to 40 minutes until golden brown.

5. Using a fork, scrape and fluff the squash strands starting from the outer edges of the squash until it turns into "spaghetti" strands.

one-pan moroccan chickpeas

SERVES 6

If you haven't made Moroccan-style chickpeas before, you are in for a treat. The sweet and savory combination of the spices, chickpeas, dried apricots, and tomatoes make for a harmony of flavors. I suggest pairing this warm, hearty chickpea dish with the Golden Goddess Spiced Rice (page 190) because they work so well together.

prep time:
5 minutes

cook time:
25 minutes

1 tbsp olive oil

1 cup diced yellow onion

3 cloves garlic, minced

½ tsp ground cumin

½ tsp ground cinnamon

1 tsp paprika

½ tsp coriander

¼ tsp ginger

½ tsp salt

¼ tsp pepper

1 (14 oz) can diced tomatoes

½ cup diced dried apricots

2 (15 oz) cans chickpeas, rinsed and drained

3 tbsp tomato paste

¾ cup veggie broth

1. Heat a large pan to medium heat.

2. Once heated, add the olive oil, onion, and garlic. Sauté for a few minutes until golden.

3. Add the spices and sauté for another minute.

4. Pour in the tomatoes, apricots, chickpeas, tomato paste, and veggie broth. Stir until well combined.

5. Cover and simmer for 20 minutes.

golden goddess spiced rice

SERVES 6

Meet your new favorite way to make rice. It's an elevated rice recipe that will impress anyone you make it for. The spices, in combination with the coconut milk, give this rice the most-incredible flavor. I recommend pairing this rice with the One-Pan Moroccan Chickpeas (page 189) as it complements that dish perfectly.

prep time:
5 minutes

cook time:
15 minutes

2 tbsp olive oil

1 tsp coriander

½ tsp ground cumin

1½ tsp turmeric

¼ tsp pepper

½ tsp salt, plus more to taste

1 tsp garlic powder

1 cup jasmine rice

2 cups water

1 cup full-fat coconut milk

1. Heat a pot to medium heat, and add the olive oil, spices, and rice. Sauté and stir for a few minutes. This toasts the rice and allows the spices to become more fragrant.

2. Pour in the water and coconut milk. Bring to a boil, then cover and simmer for 15 minutes until the rice is tender.

garlic rosemary roasted potatoes

SERVES 5

Roasting potatoes is cooking 101. Knowing how to make a pan of roasted potatoes is a must. It's so simple, yet it always impresses the people you serve it to.

prep time:
10 minutes

cook time:
30 minutes

1½ lb fingerling potatoes, cut in half lengthwise

1 tbsp minced garlic

2 tbsp olive oil

1 tbsp chopped fresh rosemary

1 tsp chopped fresh thyme

1 tsp salt

¼ tsp pepper

Fresh parsley for garnish

1. Preheat the oven to 400°F (200°C), and line a baking sheet with parchment paper.

2. In a large bowl, combine the potatoes, garlic, olive oil, rosemary, thyme, salt, and pepper. Mix well.

3. Pour the potatoes onto the prepared baking sheet, and spread evenly.

4. Bake for 30 minutes, stirring halfway through, until the potatoes are golden and tender.

HealthyGirl Tip
Keep the skin on the potatoes, as there are nutrients in the skin that have great health benefits.

best vegan mashed potatoes ever

SERVES 6–8

Creamy, rich, garlicky, vegan mashed potatoes are too good to be true. When you use almond milk, vegan butter, and nutritional yeast, you can make dairy-free mashed potatoes that you'd never guess weren't loaded with heavy cream. Not only are these a better-for-you version, they also taste super indulgent.

prep time:
5 minutes

cook time:
30 minutes

5 cloves garlic, peeled

6 medium Yukon Gold potatoes

½ cup unsweetened, plain almond milk

2 tbsp vegan butter

2 tbsp nutritional yeast

1 tsp salt

¼ tsp pepper

Chives for garnish

1. Preheat the oven to 400°F (200°C).

2. Wrap the garlic in foil, and bake for 15 minutes or until soft.

3. While the garlic roasts, peel and cut the potatoes, then add them into a large pot. Add water to the pot to cover the potatoes.

4. Bring the potatoes to a boil, and cook for 15 minutes until they are fork-tender.

5. Drain the potatoes and add them back into the pot.

6. Pour in the almond milk, and mash with a potato masher.

7. In a small bowl, mash the garlic with a fork until it forms a paste.

8. Add the garlic, vegan butter, nutritional yeast, salt, and pepper to the potatoes. Mash until smooth.

9. Garnish with fresh chives and serve!

HealthyGirl Tip

Don't have any fresh garlic cloves? Add 1 teaspoon garlic powder to the potatoes instead!

healthygirl hosting

impress everyone you know

vegan grazing board

SERVES 6–8

Charcuterie boards typically have meat and cheese on them, but this is a fully plant-based board. When it comes to making a perfectly balanced board, you need a mix of crunchy, creamy, salty, savory, and sweet. My board is just an example, so when you make your own board, you can choose from any crackers, breads, fresh fruits, dried fruits, veggies, olives, nuts, seeds, mustards, jams, dips, and vegan cheeses.

prep time:
20 minutes

Board ideas:

Vegan cheeses

Hummus

Whole-grain crackers

Water crackers

Cucumbers

Radishes

Cauliflower

Cornichon pickles

Olives

Grapes

Dried apricots

Salted almonds

Pistachios

1. Place your vegan cheeses and dips down first, and then build the rest of the board around these centerpiece items.

2. Add the different kinds of crackers or bread around the cheeses and dips.

3. Add veggies, a bowl of olives, and fruit, and fill in the gaps with nuts!

> **HealthyGirl Tip**
> There is no right or wrong way to make a board. Have fun and get creative!

mini caprese skewers

MAKES 15

There's nothing like a caprese salad. It's light, fresh, and perfect for hosting. Instead of making a caprese salad, try making these skewers instead. This style of serving makes it easier for guests to grab a skewer as they please. These are beyond simple to make, but they look so elegant and fancy.

prep time:
15 minutes

1 block firm tofu, cubed

2 cups cherry tomatoes

1 cup basil leaves

3 tbsp olive oil

3 tbsp balsamic glaze

Salt and pepper, to taste

1. Assemble the skewers by adding on the tomato first, followed by a basil leaf, a tofu cube, another basil leaf, then another tomato. Repeat until all ingredients are used.

2. Add the skewers onto a platter as you make them.

3. Drizzle the olive oil and balsamic glaze over top and season with salt and pepper.

HealthyGirl Tip
4-inch appetizer skewers work perfectly for these!

buffalo cauliflower poppers

SERVES 5

If you need a super-easy appetizer that everyone will enjoy, buffalo cauliflower poppers are going to be your new favorite. They are perfect for game day, birthday parties, snacking with friends—you name it. Let's be honest, no one has time to make buffalo sauce from scratch. This recipe is so simple because you can use store-bought buffalo sauce.

prep time:
5 minutes

cook time:
30 minutes

1 head cauliflower

1 tbsp cornstarch

1 tsp garlic powder

Salt and pepper, to taste

⅓ cup buffalo sauce

2 tbsp bread crumbs

Hempseed Ranch Dressing (page 76)

1. Preheat the oven to 425°F (220°C), and line a baking sheet with parchment paper.

2. Cut the cauliflower into florets. Rinse the florets in a strainer, then shake off the excess water.

3. Toss the cauliflower in a bowl with the cornstarch, garlic powder, salt, and pepper. Once evenly coated, lay on the prepared baking sheet.

4. Bake for 30 minutes or until golden brown.

5. Place the cauliflower back in the bowl and toss with buffalo sauce and bread crumbs.

6. Remove the parchment paper from the baking sheet, and place the cauliflower directly on the baking sheet. Place on the top rack of the oven, and broil for 5 minutes.

7. Pair with Hempseed Ranch Dressing and enjoy!

HealthyGirl Tip

If you want these to be crispier, make them in an air fryer instead of the oven! They will take about 15 minutes in an air fryer. Place the poppers back in the air fryer for 5 minutes after saucing.

10-minute mango salsa

SERVES 5

Fruit takes salsa to the next level. Typically, salsa is made with a tomato base, but my version is made with fresh, ripe, juicy mangoes. This is one of those appetizers that your guests will think you bought at the store. Pair this salsa with the Black Bean Babe Tacos (page 171) for a wonderful meal.

prep time:
10 minutes

2 cups diced ripe mango

1 red bell pepper, diced

¾ cup diced red onion

1 tbsp diced jalapeño

¼ cup chopped cilantro

2 tbsp lime juice

Salt, to taste

1 bag tortilla chips

1. Add the mango, bell pepper, onion, jalapeño, and cilantro into a bowl.

2. Drizzle on the lime juice, and season with salt to taste.

3. Serve with tortilla chips and enjoy!

gf **sf** **lf**

baked spinach artichoke dip

SERVES 8

When you make this, don't plan on having leftovers because the casserole dish will be licked clean. There is nothing like some warm, creamy, indulgent spinach artichoke dip served with high-quality crusty bread. This is one of those dips that is great to bring with you to someone else's house. Just ask them to warm it up in their oven before serving it!

prep time:
10 minutes

cook time:
30 minutes

1 cup diced yellow onion

5 cloves garlic, minced

1 tbsp olive oil

1 (16 oz) package frozen spinach, defrosted and chopped

2 cans artichokes in water, drained and chopped

For the sauce:

1 cup raw cashews

½ block firm tofu

1 clove garlic

¼ cup nutritional yeast

1 cup almond milk

Juice of ½ lemon

1 tsp salt

¼ tsp pepper

1. Preheat the oven to 425°F (220°C). You can use a large cast-iron skillet so you can transfer the dip directly into the oven, or use a casserole dish.

2. Heat the skillet to medium, and add the onion, garlic, and olive oil. Sauté for a few minutes.

3. Add the spinach and artichokes to the skillet, and sauté on medium to high heat until all the moisture is cooked out, about 15 minutes.

4. For the creamy sauce, add the cashews, tofu, 1 garlic clove, nutritional yeast, almond milk, lemon juice, salt, and pepper into a high-speed blender. Blend until completely smooth, scraping down the sides once or twice.

5. Pour the sauce into the spinach mixture, and stir to combine thoroughly.

6. Place the cast-iron skillet into the oven. (Or transfer to a casserole dish, then place in the oven.) Bake for 15 minutes or until golden brown on top.

7. Serve warm with bread, chips, or veggies and enjoy!

air-fryer falafel + israeli salad

SERVES 5

It's actually super easy to make a healthier version of falafel at home—just use your air fryer. I am a falafel girlie through and through, but because they're fried, they typically give me heartburn. This air-fryer version with Israeli salad is delish. Stuff these inside a pita pocket with hummus, Israeli salad, and tahini. You'll thank me later.

prep time:
50 minutes

cook time:
10 minutes

Falafel:

2 (15 oz) cans chickpeas, rinsed and drained

1 cup fresh parsley, stems removed

1 cup fresh cilantro, stems removed

1 white onion, quartered

4 cloves garlic

1 tsp salt

½ tsp pepper

1 tbsp ground cumin

1 tbsp coriander

1 tsp baking powder

2 tbsp sesame seeds

Olive oil

Israeli salad:

2 cups quartered cherry tomatoes

2 cups diced cucumbers

½ cup diced red onion

1 tbsp lemon juice

Salt and pepper, to taste

Optional toppings:

Hummus

Tahini

Cabbage slaw

1. Add the chickpeas, parsley, cilantro, onion, garlic, salt, pepper, cumin, and coriander into a food processor. Blend in 30-second increments until completely combined, scraping down the sides as necessary.

2. Put the chickpea mixture into a bowl and refrigerate for 30 minutes.

3. Remove the mixture from the fridge. Add the baking powder into the bowl and mix. Add the sesame seeds and mix again.

4. Scoop the batter and form into patties about ½ inch thick and 2 inches wide.

5. Arrange the falafel on the air-fryer tray. Leave space between them. (You might need to do a few batches.)

6. Spray both sides of the falafel with olive oil spray or brush with olive oil.

7. Air fry at 400°F (200°C) for 10 minutes or until golden brown.

8. While these air fry, prepare the Israeli salad. Add the tomato, cucumber, and red onion to a bowl, then stir in the lemon juice and salt and pepper.

9. Serve the falafel with the salad in a pita pocket, or as is with optional toppings.

bite-size deviled potatoes

MAKES 30

I am sure you've had deviled eggs, but have you tried making deviled potatoes? When I serve these to guests, they are a massive hit every time. (Everyone loves finger food!) I recommend these as a daytime appetizer. The hearty potato pairs perfectly with the creamy center that's reminiscent of an egg yolk. Take this as your sign to make these the next time you host!

prep time:
15 minutes

cook time:
20 minutes

15 small Yukon Gold potatoes

3 tbsp yellow mustard

2 tbsp vegan mayo or plain dairy-free yogurt

1½ tsp white wine vinegar

1 tsp salt

½ tsp turmeric

Garnish:

Paprika

Dill

Chives

1. Bring a large pot of water to a boil.

2. Boil the potatoes whole for 20 minutes or until completely cooked. You should be able to push a toothpick through with ease. Do not overcook.

3. Strain and add the potatoes into a bowl with ice and water to cool them down. Strain again after 5 minutes. Cut in half.

4. Scoop a well into the center of each potato half with a teaspoon. Add the potato scoops into a bowl to make the filling.

5. To make the filling, use the scooped-out potato, mustard, mayo, white wine vinegar, salt, and turmeric. Mash and mix until completely smooth. Add more mayo if it's too thick.

6. Add the filling into a piping bag or zip-top bag with a corner snipped off. Fill each potato well with the filling.

7. Garnish with paprika, dill, and chives.

8. Keep the leftovers refrigerated to enjoy later.

whole-grain dinner rolls (with herb oil)

MAKES 12

There is nothing quite like homemade bread. In fact, I think the best part of going to a restaurant is when they bring you warm bread with a great dipping oil as an appetizer. It's the ideal situation. These rolls are super easy to make at home and are a great addition to any dinner party!

prep time:
30 minutes

cook time:
15 minutes

1 tbsp rapid-rise yeast

1½ cups warm water

4 cups whole wheat flour

2 tsp salt

4 tsp cane sugar

1½ tbsp maple syrup

1 tbsp olive oil

Herb oil:

¼ cup olive oil

¼ cup fresh basil

½ tsp garlic powder

⅛ tsp red pepper flakes

1 tsp dried oregano

¼ tsp fresh thyme

Pinch of pepper

1. Preheat the oven to 425°F (220°C) and line a baking sheet with parchment paper.

2. In a small bowl, combine the yeast and water. Add the flour, salt, sugar, and maple syrup into a large mixing bowl. Pour in the activated yeast, and mix.

3. Knead by hand for about 5 to 10 minutes until the dough forms a smooth, slightly sticky ball that springs back a bit when poked with a finger.

4. Add the olive oil to another bowl, then roll the dough in the oil. Cover the bowl with a warm damp towel. Let it rise for 45 minutes in a warm place, like beside a sunny window.

5. Cut the dough into 12 equal sections, then roll into balls.

6. Place the dough balls 1 inch apart on the prepared baking sheet. Bake for 15 minutes or until golden.

7. While they bake, make the herb oil by mixing all the herb oil ingredients together in a bowl.

8. Brush the herb oil on the rolls, or keep it on the side for dipping.

summer rolls

MAKES 15

Summer Rolls—or sometimes called fresh spring rolls—are of Vietnamese origin. One of my favorite Vietnamese restaurants serves them, but I love making my own at home because I can add whatever ingredients I want to them. Once you get the hang of rolling them up, they are super fun to make. They are crispy, crunchy, light, and fresh. Try having a summer roll-making party with your guests and get everyone involved!

prep time:
30 minutes

2 packages rice paper wrappers

10–15 green leaf lettuce leaves

1 fresh mango, sliced

1 red bell pepper, sliced

1 large cucumber, thinly sliced

2 avocados, thinly sliced

2 cups thinly sliced purple cabbage

1 cup chopped cilantro

2 cups carrot ribbons

½ cup fresh mint leaves

Sesame seeds for garnish

Dreamy dipping sauce:

½ cup tahini

¼ cup coconut aminos

1 tbsp toasted sesame oil

1 tbsp lime juice

1. Rinse a rice paper wrapper in warm water for 5 seconds then lay it on a cutting board. Layer the fillings in the center of the wrapper, starting with the green leaf lettuce. Don't overstuff.

2. Roll tightly like a burrito by bringing the side of the wrapper closest to you over the ingredients, folding in each side, then rolling up the rest. Cut in half with a sharp knife or serve it whole.

3. Repeat until all the ingredients are used.

4. To make the sauce, mix all the ingredients in a bowl until well combined.

5. Garnish the rolls with sesame seeds, then serve immediately while they're fresh!

hearts of palm crab cakes

MAKES 12

I have a mental list of my favorite recipes I've ever created, and this is definitely in the top ten. I didn't think it was possible to have crab cakes without the crab, but chickpeas and hearts of palm make it doable. You'll be surprised at how incredibly delicious these vegan crab cakes are.

prep time:
20 minutes

cook time:
15 minutes

1 (15 oz) can chickpeas

⅓ cup aquafaba (chickpea can liquid)

2 cans hearts of palm, drained

1½ cups bread crumbs, divided

2 tsp lemon juice

2 tsp Dijon mustard

1 tsp Old Bay Seasoning

½ tsp salt

1 tsp garlic powder

1 tsp hot sauce

1 tbsp vegan mayo

1 tbsp olive oil

Garnish:
Fresh parsley
Lemon wedge

Vegan aioli:
1 cup vegan mayo
1–2 tbsp hot sauce

1. Drain the chickpeas, but reserve ⅓ cup of the liquid (aquafaba). Pulse the chickpeas and hearts of palm in a food processor. Do not overblend.

2. In a bowl, mix together the aquafaba, 1 cup of the bread crumbs, lemon juice, mustard, Old Bay, salt, garlic powder, hot sauce, and vegan mayo.

3. Add the mixture of chickpeas and hearts of palm mixture to the bowl and combine.

4. Form into patties about 3 to 4 inches in diameter.

5. Add the remaining bread crumbs onto a plate. Roll the patties in the bread crumbs.

6. Panfry in the olive oil on medium heat for 4 minutes on each side or until golden brown. (Refresh the olive oil in the pan as necessary.)

7. To make the aioli, mix the vegan mayo and hot sauce in a small bowl and serve with the crab cakes. Garnish with fresh parsley and lemon wedge, and enjoy!

build-your-own sushi bowl

SERVES 5

Sushi bowls (aka deconstructed sushi rolls) are going to be your new favorite hosting meal because everyone has a blast making their own bowl. I suggest putting each ingredient and topping in its own bowl so your guests can make their sushi bowls easily. This way, everyone can make a custom bowl suitable to whatever they like.

prep time:
20 minutes

cook time:
20 minutes

Sushi rice:

1 cup short-grain rice

2 tbsp rice vinegar

Toppings:

2 cups chopped or thinly sliced cucumbers

2 avocados, sliced

2 cups shredded carrots

1 cup kimchi

8 shredded or quartered nori sheets

2 cups steamed shelled edamame

Tofu:

1 tbsp sesame oil

1 block extra-firm tofu

2 tbsp coconut aminos or soy sauce

Garnish:

Sesame seeds

Pickled ginger

Wasabi

1. To make quick, flavorful sushi rice, make short-grain rice according to the box instructions. When it's done, fluff with a fork and add rice vinegar.

2. Place the cucumbers, avocados, carrots, kimchi, nori, edamame, sesame seeds, pickled ginger, and wasabi into separate small bowls.

3. Cut the tofu into cubes. Sauté in the sesame oil on medium heat, stirring every 30 seconds, until golden brown. Once golden, turn the heat down to a simmer and add the coconut aminos. Sauté and mix the tofu until combined with the coconut aminos.

4. Place the tofu in a small bowl as well, and arrange all the bowls together so your guests can build their own sushi bowls. Serve with chopsticks and have fun!

HealthyGirl Tip

Shred the nori if you want to sprinkle it on top of the bowls, or cut the nori sheets into quarters if you want guests to be able to add their bowl ingredients to the nori as they eat to make mini handheld rolls.

---

gf sf nf lf

holiday favorite shepherd's pie

SERVES 8

If you've been looking for a meatless main course for a big event or holiday dinner, stop right here because this shepherd's pie is absolutely to die for. It really gives those meat-and-potatoes vibes that people crave for a holiday feast. It's made with lentils, which means it's hearty, filling, and protein-packed. I've made this for vegans and meat-eaters and they gobble it up.

prep time:
15 minutes

cook time:
30 minutes

1 yellow onion, diced

1 cup chopped carrots

1½ cups diced baby bella mushrooms

1 tbsp olive oil

1 cup frozen peas

½ tsp fresh or dried thyme

1 tbsp chopped fresh parsley

1 tsp dried or fresh rosemary

1 tsp salt

¼ tsp pepper

½ cup red wine

1 (6 oz) can tomato paste

3 cups cooked canned lentils, rinsed and drained

1½ cups veggie broth

1 batch **Best Vegan Mashed Potatoes Ever** (pg 194)

1. Preheat the oven to 425°F (220°C).

2. In a large sauté pan, on medium to high heat, sauté the onion, carrots, and mushrooms in olive oil until cooked down and soft, 5 to 8 minutes, then add the frozen peas.

3. Add the thyme, parsley, rosemary, salt, and pepper.

4. Sauté for another few minutes then deglaze the pan with the red wine. Let the wine reduce for a few minutes.

5. Add the tomato paste, cooked lentils, and veggie broth. Simmer on low heat for 5 more minutes, stirring until combined. Turn off the heat, and pour into a 9 x 13-inch casserole dish.

6. Top the lentil base with the Best Vegan Mashed Potatoes Ever. Place dollops of the mashed potatoes on top and gently spread.

7. Bake for 10 minutes on the middle rack, then broil on the top rack for 5 minutes or until the top is golden brown.

beauty beet + bean burgers

MAKES 7

These are hands-down going to be the most delicious homemade veggie burgers you've ever had. Made with a base of quinoa, beans, and beets, these superfood, vitamin-rich ingredients are amazing for your skin, your hair, and your overall health. They are smoky, hearty, savory, filling, and take less than 30 minutes to make.

prep time:
10 minutes

cook time:
15 minutes

1 cup chopped white onion

1 tbsp olive oil

1 cup pecans

1 tbsp smoked paprika

1 tbsp chili powder

1 tbsp garlic powder

1 tsp salt

½ tsp pepper

1 cup cooked quinoa

⅓ cup bread crumbs

1 (15 oz) can black beans, rinsed and drained

2 small, precooked beets (jarred, store-bought)

⅓ cup BBQ sauce

1. Sauté the onions in a pan on medium heat with olive oil until translucent. Remove from the heat.

2. In a food processor, add the pecans, smoked paprika, chili powder, garlic powder, salt, and pepper, and blend until combined.

3. Pour the onions, cooked quinoa, bread crumbs, and pecan mixture into a large bowl.

4. Add the black beans and beets into the food processor, and blend to combine. Don't overblend, as there should still be a little bit of texture present.

5. Pour the bean mixture into the bowl as well, along with the BBQ sauce. Mix until well combined.

6. Form into patties, it should yield about 7.

7. Panfry on medium heat for about 4 to 5 minutes on each side, or grill them.

8. Serve on a bun with your favorite burger toppings.

crowd-pleasing red pepper pasta

SERVES 5

This crowd-pleasing red pepper pasta is next level. Not only does the sauce have hidden nutrient-dense red bell peppers, but it's beyond easy to make. Hosting tip: when you make pasta for guests, try finding a unique pasta shape, as it elevates your dish. I found this fun pasta shape, called calamarata, and it makes the dish look restaurant worthy.

prep time:
10 minutes

cook time:
30 minutes

2 red bell peppers, seeded and roughly chopped

1 cup chopped yellow onion

3 cloves garlic

Olive oil spray

1 tsp salt

¼ tsp pepper

1 (16 oz) package pasta

2 tbsp tahini

2 tbsp nutritional yeast

1 cup unsweetened almond milk

½ cup slivered almonds or raw cashews

Garnish:

Fresh basil

Vegan parmesan

Red pepper flakes

1. Preheat the oven to 425°F (220°C), and line a baking sheet with parchment paper.

2. Add the peppers, onion, and garlic cloves to the prepared baking sheet. Spray with olive oil spray, and season with salt and pepper. Roast for 20 to 30 minutes.

3. Bring a large pot of water to a boil. Salt the pasta water and cook the pasta according to the package instructions.

4. While the pasta cooks, add the roasted peppers, onion, and garlic into a blender, along with the tahini, nutritional yeast, almond milk, almonds, salt, and pepper. Blend until smooth.

5. Strain the pasta (save some pasta water), add the pasta back into the pot on low heat, and pour the sauce and a little pasta water in to add richness to the sauce. Stir then serve! Garnish with fresh basil, vegan parmesan, and red pepper flakes.

healthygirl desserts

sweet treats to enjoy without guilt

1-ingredient mango sorbet

SERVES 2

Craving something sweet and refreshing, but need something that takes less than 5 minutes to make? Mango sorbet is going to be your new dessert BFF. I recommend keeping bags of frozen mango on hand so you can make this anytime. Don't like mangoes? This pretty much works with any frozen fruit. Just add the frozen fruit of your choice to your food processor (with no liquid), and blend until smooth!

prep time:
5 minutes

2 cups frozen mango

Fresh mint for garnish

1. Blend frozen mango in a food processor until smooth. Scrape down the sides every 45 seconds. This process will take about 5 minutes.

2. Keep scraping until a sorbet is formed.

3. Scoop into a bowl and garnish with fresh mint. So refreshing!

strawberry shortcake bars

MAKES 9

This is going to be one of the best desserts you'll ever put in your mouth, I am not exaggerating. These strawberry shortcake bars are buttery, melt-in-your-mouth, perfectly sweet, and taste like a warm strawberry cake mixed with a cookie bar and muffin, all at once. Ten out of ten.

prep time:
10 minutes

cook time:
20 minutes

1 tbsp cornstarch

¼ cup almond milk

⅓ cup melted vegan butter

2 tbsp agave

⅓ cup cane or coconut sugar

1 tsp lemon juice

1 tsp pure vanilla extract

1¾ cups almond flour

¼ cup coconut flour

¼ tsp baking soda

Pinch of salt

1 cup diced strawberries

⅓ cup vegan white chocolate chips

Freeze dried strawberries for garnish

1. Preheat the oven to 350°F (175°C). Line a 9 x 9-inch baking pan with parchment paper.

2. In a medium bowl, whisk together the cornstarch and almond milk. Add the melted butter, agave, sugar, lemon juice, and vanilla. Mix to combine.

3. Add the almond flour, coconut flour, baking soda, and salt. Mix with a spoon until a dough forms. Stir in the diced strawberries. Pour the dough into the pan and press down until even.

4. Bake for 15 to 18 minutes or until the edges are golden brown. Let cool for 30 minutes. Melt the white chocolate chips, then spread it on top. Sprinkle on the freeze-dried strawberries.

5. Let them sit in the freezer for 10 minutes, then carefully cut into bars.

peachy peach crisp

SERVES 8

This warm, heavenly peach crisp is not only easy and healthy, but it's also one of those desserts you're going to have on repeat. Peaches are in season during the summer months, but if you want to make this year-round and can't find good peaches, you can always replace the peaches with apples or berries!

prep time:
15 minutes

cook time:
30 minutes

Crumble topping:

½ cup rolled oats

½ cup almond flour

⅓ cup coconut sugar

⅓ cup macadamia oil

½ cup raw walnuts

¼ cup shredded coconut

1 tsp pure vanilla extract

2 tsp ground cinnamon

Pinch of sea salt

Filling:

7 peaches (about 6 cups
    of fruit)

¼ cup coconut sugar

1 tbsp potato starch or
    cornstarch

1 tsp lemon juice

1. Preheat the oven to 350°F (175°C).

2. Put the crumble topping ingredients in a food processor, and pulse until combined.

3. Cut the peaches into slices, and mix together with the other filling ingredients in a large bowl.

4. Add the filling to a 9 x 9-inch baking dish, and top with the crumble topping.

5. Bake for 30 minutes or until bubbly and golden brown.

6. Serve with vanilla ice cream. So good!

frozen banana chocolate pops

MAKES 6

If you're like me, you're always reaching for dessert after dinner. There's something about needing to cap off the night with something sweet. I like to keep a batch of these in my freezer at all times for a quick, healthy, frozen treat.

prep time:
10 minutes

3 bananas

¾ cup dark chocolate chips

Topping ideas:

Shredded coconut

Chopped nuts

Cacao nibs or mini chocolate chips

Sprinkles

1. Line a baking sheet or a platter with parchment paper.

2. Peel and cut each banana in half, crosswise.

3. Add the chocolate chips to a microwave-safe bowl, and heat for 45 seconds at a time until completely melted. Pour into a mason jar or tall glass—this will make dipping easier.

4. Stick a wooden skewer into each banana half, dip each in melted chocolate, and lay flat on the prepared baking sheet.

5. Sprinkle the bananas with the desired toppings and freeze.

6. Freeze for at least 3 hours before eating. These last in the freezer for up to a month!

pecan pie bars

MAKES 9

In my humble opinion, there are two desserts that need to be on the fall holiday dinner table: pumpkin pie and pecan pie. Pecan pie bars are a fun way to make a traditional pecan pie with a twist. Once you cut them into bars, everyone can pick them up and eat with their hands! These taste exactly like a classic pecan pie, but with healthier ingredients.

prep time:
10 minutes

cook time:
40 minutes

Crust:

1½ cups almond flour

2 tbsp maple syrup

3 tbsp melted coconut oil or vegan butter

1 tsp pure vanilla extract

Filling:

3 tbsp potato starch or cornstarch

¾ cup full-fat coconut milk

1½ cups pecans

½ cup coconut sugar

⅓ cup maple syrup

1 tsp pure vanilla extract

1. Preheat the oven to 350°F (175°C). Line a 9 x 9-inch baking sheet with parchment paper.

2. Make the crust by mixing all of the crust ingredients together in a bowl until it forms a dough. Press it down evenly in the bottom of the pan. Bake for 7 minutes. Let cool for 20 minutes.

3. While it cools, make the pecan pie filling. Combine the potato starch and coconut milk in a bowl and whisk.

4. In a pan, dry toast the pecans on medium heat for 1 minute until warmed. Turn down the heat to low, and add the coconut sugar, maple syrup, and vanilla. Stir, then add the coconut milk and potato starch mixture. Stir until smooth.

5. Spread the pecan pie mixture evenly over top of the almond flour crust.

6. Bake for 30 minutes. Cool for a few hours, then let set in the fridge overnight or for at least 8 hours.

7. Serve the next day, and enjoy with whipped cream or vanilla ice cream.

no-bake coconut caramel cookie bars

MAKES 9

So, long story short, I was a Girl Scout when I was little. I 100 percent stayed in it for the free cookies. My favorite Girl Scout cookie is the Samoa. It's perfection. I wanted to create my own cookie bar that tasted exactly like this beloved cookie.

prep time:
10 minutes

cook time:
1 hour

1 cup toasted shredded coconut

½ cup rolled oats

1 cup pitted Medjool dates (about 12)

1 tsp pure vanilla extract

¼ tsp salt

¾ cup dark chocolate chips

1. Toast the coconut shreds in a pan on medium heat, stirring constantly, until golden brown for about 5 minutes.

2. Add the coconut into a food processor. Add the oats, and blend for 30 seconds.

3. Add the dates, vanilla, and salt. Blend until completely combined.

4. In a loaf pan lined with parchment paper, press the cookie mixture into the bottom in an even layer.

5. Melt the dark chocolate in the microwave in 30-second increments until fully melted.

6. Pour the chocolate over the top of the cookie base. Freeze for 1 hour, then cut into bars. Refrigerate the rest.

(gf) (sf) (nf) (lf)

hot chocolate cookies

MAKES 8

If you like drinking hot chocolate, stop here and make these 1-bowl hot chocolate cookies. They taste exactly like hot chocolate in cookie form. The rich, fudgy cookie with the gooey marshmallow on top will seriously make you drool.

prep time:
15 minutes

cook time:
15 minutes

2 tbsp ground flaxseed

5 tbsp water

¼ cup chocolate chips

¼ cup unsalted vegan butter, melted

½ cup coconut sugar

1 tsp pure vanilla extract

¼ cup cocoa

½ cup gluten-free flour

½ cup almond flour

¼ tsp baking powder

¼ tsp baking soda

Pinch of salt

9 pieces of a milk chocolate bar

5 large vegan marshmallows cut in half

1. Preheat the oven to 350°F (175°C). Line a baking sheet with parchment paper.

2. Make a flax egg by combining the ground flaxseed and water. Set aside and let sit for 5 minutes.

3. To a large microwave-safe bowl, add the chocolate chips and butter. Melt for 30 seconds, then mix.

4. Add the coconut sugar, vanilla, and flax egg, then mix.

5. Add the cocoa, gluten-free flour, almond flour, baking powder, baking soda, and salt, then mix. Scoop onto the prepared baking sheet in ¼-cup scoops spaced 3 inches apart.

6. Bake for 7 to 8 minutes. Add 1 piece of a chocolate bar to the center of each cookie, pressing down slightly. Add half of a large marshmallow to each. Bake for another 5 to 6 minutes.

7. Let cool for 10 minutes, then enjoy.

edible cookie dough

SERVES 6

Let's be honest, the cookie dough is better than the actual cookies. The best part about vegan cookie dough is that you don't need to worry about raw eggs. This cookie dough is made from chickpeas, and you'd never know it. It's packed with fiber and protein, and is the perfect sweet treat.

prep time:
10 minutes

cook time:
2 hours

1 (15 oz) can chickpeas, rinsed and drained

5 Medjool dates

½ cup creamy peanut butter

¼ cup rolled oats

¼ cup coconut sugar

¼ cup maple syrup

1 tsp pure vanilla extract

½ cup vegan chocolate chips, plus more for topping

Sea salt for garnish

1. In a food processor, combine the chickpeas, dates, peanut butter, oats, sugar, syrup, and vanilla, and blend until smooth.

2. Transfer the mixture to a medium bowl and fold in the chocolate chips.

3. Sprinkle on more chocolate chips and sea salt for topping.

4. Refrigerate for at least 2 hours before enjoying.

HealthyGirl Tip
Eat it by the spoonful; it's the best way!

homemade butterfingers

MAKES 12

If Halloween was always one of your favorite holidays because you got to eat a ton of Butterfingers, I'm with you. These no-bake, homemade butterfingers are made with better-for-you ingredients, but taste like the real deal. They're crunchy and crispy in the middle and perfectly sweet from the dark chocolate on the outside.

prep time:
30 minutes

cook time:
10 minutes

3 cups natural cornflakes

1 cup smooth peanut butter

⅓ cup maple syrup

Pinch of sea salt

1¼ cups melted dark chocolate

1. Grind the cornflakes in a food processor until they resemble crumbs.

2. In a bowl, mix the peanut butter with the maple syrup and salt.

3. Add the cornflakes crumbs into the peanut butter mixture.

4. Form into little bars, and add onto a baking sheet lined with parchment paper.

5. Set in the freezer for 10 to 15 minutes.

6. Melt the dark chocolate chips in the microwave in 30-second increments, stirring in between.

7. Dip the bars in the chocolate, then let set in the fridge for 15 minutes.

famous chickpea brownies

MAKES 9

If there was one recipe I had to include in this cookbook, it was going to be my famous chickpea brownies. These have the richness and indulgence of a traditional brownie, but healthier-for-you ingredients. Guess what? You can't taste the chickpeas at all.

prep time:
10 minutes

cook time:
25 minutes

1 (15 oz) can chickpeas, rinsed and drained

½ cup almond butter or peanut butter

¼ cup oat or almond flour

¼ cup cocoa powder

½ cup maple syrup

1 tbsp applesauce

1 tsp pure vanilla extract

¼ tsp baking soda

¼ tsp baking powder

¼ tsp pink salt

½ cup vegan chocolate chips, plus ⅓ cup for topping

1. Preheat the oven to 350°F (175°C). Line a 9 x 9-inch baking pan with parchment paper.

2. Add all the ingredients—except the chocolate chips—into a food processor. Blend until completely smooth.

3. Fold in the chocolate chips, then pour into the prepared baking dish. Top with the extra chocolate chips.

4. Bake for 20 to 25 minutes. When they are done, let them cool for about 20 minutes before cutting into them.

Acknowledgments

Ever since the inception of the HealthyGirl Kitchen brand, writing a cookbook was the dream. I always keep a list of goals that remind me of my purpose and "write a cookbook" came in as my top goal. I'll never forget the day I received an email from my amazing editor, Alexander Rigby, who wanted to bring the *HealthyGirl Kitchen* cookbook to life. Not only was my dream of writing a cookbook going to come true, but I'd do it with the #1 publisher in the world, and for that I couldn't be prouder.

First and foremost, I'd like to thank my best friend who also happens be my husband, Ari. Thank you for being my recipe tester even when you weren't hungry, for doing the dishes when I was too tired, for allowing me to convert your office into a photo studio, for working from home for months so you could take on the very high-pressure job of being the lead photographer of the book, and most importantly, for encouraging and supporting my dreams more than anyone else. I know I tell you 100 times a day, but I love you!

And to my incredible management team, for representing me, and the HealthyGirl Kitchen brand, you've helped bring my cookbook dreams to fruition. To one of the hardest working people I've ever met, my agent and bad-ass manager, Christina Brennan, thank you for believing in me.

Taylor, you started out as my trusted assistant, and I am so lucky to now call you a good friend. I can wholeheartedly say the book would not have been possible without your help. From the grocery shopping, to figuring out how to stuff the insane amount of ingredients and leftovers into my small fridge, to helping me test every single recipe, you were the best cookbook partner in crime. Talia, I also want to thank you for coming to my rescue on the days I needed a little extra help.

Mom and Dad, I know being a food and lifestyle influencer and CEO of my own brand is far from traditional, but I genuinely am so grateful for your unwavering support, for letting me watch Food Network for hours as a kid while pretending I was Rachael Ray, and for never questioning my unique path. Bob and Greta, my in-laws, thank you for eating at least half of the recipe-testing leftovers and for being the best cheerleaders.

Working with the DK team at Penguin Random House has been an incredible experience. I couldn't have asked for a more dedicated, patient, organized, and talented group of people who from the beginning, believed in the *HealthyGirl Kitchen* cookbook vision as much as I did. I know I am a bit of a perfectionist, but they have truly made this book perfect.

Of course, I must thank my HealthyGirl community, my followers and fans who have been on this journey with me for quite some time. I know you have been waiting very patiently for this book. I can't wait for you to finally get your hands on it. I hope you use this book in good health, share it with friends and family, and find a permanent spot for it on your kitchen counter as it helps you fall in love with cooking and nourishing your body.

With love,
Danielle

Index